The
WISDOM
of
HINDUISM

OTHER TITLES IN THIS SERIES

The Wisdom of Jesus, ISBN 1–85168–225–2

The Wisdom of Buddhism, ISBN 1–85168–226–0

The Wisdom of the Qur'an, ISBN 1–85168–224–4

The Wisdom of the Tao, ISBN 1–85168–232–5

The Wisdom of Judaism, ISBN 1–85168–228–7

RELATED TITLES PUBLISHED BY ONEWORLD

God's BIG Book of Virtues

God's BIG Handbook for the Soul

God's BIG Instruction Book

The Oneworld Book of Prayer

Words to Comfort, Words to Heal

The
WISDOM
of
HINDUISM

Compiled by Klaus K. Klostermaier

ONEWORLD

OXFORD

THE WISDOM OF HINDUISM
Oneworld Publications
(Sales and Editorial)
185 Banbury Road
Oxford OX2 7AR
England

http://www.oneworld-publications.com

Oneworld Publications
(US Marketing Office)
160 N Washington St.
4th Floor, Boston
MA 02114
USA

ISBN 1–85168–227–9

Cover design by Design Deluxe
Typeset by Cyclops Media Productions
Printed and bound by Graphicom Srl, Vicenza, Italy

CONTENTS

FOR DORIS

ACKNOWLEDGEMENTS

The publisher would like to thank the following institutions for assistance and permission to produce the following pictures:

Robert Harding Picture Library (pp. 37, 57, 68, 140, 168, 181); The Hutchison Library (pp. vi, 29, 89, 97, 113, 121, 153); Rasamandala Das, ISKCON Educational Services (pp. 20, 73, 80, 93, 101, 109, 132, 145, 160, 176).

PREFACE

THERE IS much in the wisdom of Hinduism that easily resonates with everyone regardless of background and culture – human experience in many ways has been much the same all over the world throughout the ages. However, there is also much in the wisdom of Hinduism, as in any other, that is particular, specific, conditioned by culture and history. Consider rebirth: Hindus have spent much ingenuity figuring out the best ways to escape from repeated rebirths and the sufferings connected with them. Wisdom relating to this issue will only make sense to someone who shares that belief.

While this anthology does reflect the wisdom of Hinduism, it is based on choices made by someone from a different culture, holding a different view of life. The wisdom of Hinduism, like all traditional wisdom, is often ambiguous and self-contradictory – as is all life. Wisdom itself must be used wisely if it is to serve as a guiding light.

KLAUS K. KLOSTERMAIER

ABOUT THE SOURCES

UNTIL FAIRLY recently Hindus did not define their tradition as "Hinduism" over against other religions but followed a great many different worship affiliations more narrowly circumscribed as Vaishnava, Shaiva, Shakta, Smarta etc. In matters of common law and social custom they mostly followed what they called *sanatana dharma*, the "eternal law", based on a timeless all-Indian tradition. Hinduism has no central authority and there is no clear demarcation within Indian literature of a "Hindu" over against other traditions. While some of the sources from which the *Wisdom of Hinduism* has been culled would be evidently "Hindu" because they promote the worship of "Hindu" deities, others are not so clearly identifiable. All of them belong to a common Indian cultural tradition, which in spite of sectarian rivalries between various forms of Hinduism, Buddhism and Jainism shows a common perception of world and humankind.

Each of the quotes of this anthology has been identified by a reference to the source from which it was drawn, but some liberty has been taken with summarizing or slightly modifying some texts. All translations from Indian languages are my own, unless otherwise indicated, and I have endeavoured to use inclusive language and to avoid archaisms. English original texts have been reproduced as they were found, while the spelling of Indian words has been standardized. The compilation was not approached as an exercise in Indological scholarship but was intended to invite reflection and to be enjoyed by everyone.

THE DIVINE

THE NATURE OF THE DIVINE

BRAHMAN IS the breath of life, Brahman is joy, Brahman is the heavens.

Chandogya Upanishad, IV, X, 4

THAT WHICH is the most subtle – this whole universe has That as its self. That is the Real. That is the Self. That you are.

Chandogya Upanishad, VI, X, 3

THERE IS an indefinable mysterious Power that pervades everything. I feel it, though I do not see it. It is this unseen Power which makes itself felt and yet defies all proof, because it is so unlike all that I perceive through my senses. And is this power benevolent or malevolent? I see it as purely benevolent. For I can see that in the midst of death life persists, in the midst of untruth truth persists, in the midst of darkness light persists. Hence I gather that God is Life, Truth, Light.

MAHATMA GANDHI: *Young India, 11 Oct. 1928*

A S THE same all-pervading ether is inside and outside a jar,
even so the eternal, all-pervasive Brahman exists in all
things.

Ashtavakra Samhita, I, 20

A S WAVES, foam and bubbles are not different from water,
even so the universe emanating from the Self is not
different from it.

Ashtavakra Samhita, II, 4

T O ME God is Truth and Love; God is ethics and morality;
God is fearlessness. God is the source of Light and Life and
yet He is above and beyond all these. God is conscience. He
is even the atheism of the atheist. For in His boundless love God
permits the atheist to live. He is the searcher of hearts. He
transcends speech and reason. He knows us and our hearts
better than we do ourselves. He does not take us at our word for
he knows that often we do not mean it, some knowingly and
others unknowingly.

MAHATMA GANDHI: *Young India, 5 Mar. 1925*

THE FREED souls as well as their world are included in Shiva. Being wholly pure, they all equally possess Shivahood. It consists in being completely different from the state of mundane existence involving endless cycles of creation and destruction. Omniscient, capable of moving everywhere, tranquil, abodes of eternal and supreme lordship, having the veils of sins destroyed completely, perceiving him everywhere, having him as their souls they attain places just as they like and having experienced all objects of desire, they shine forth with him in all places at all times.

SHRIKANTHA: *Shrikanthabhashya, end*

IN MY early youth I was taught to repeat what in Hindu scriptures are known as the one thousand names of God. But these one thousand names of God were by no means exhaustive. We believe – and I think it is the truth – that God has as many names as there are creatures and, therefore, we also say that God is nameless and, since God has many forms, we also consider Him formless, and since He speaks through many tongues, we consider Him speechless.

MAHATMA GANDHI: *Young India, 31 Dec. 1931*

MANIFEST, AND also hidden, called "moving-in-secret", the great abode. Therein is placed that which moves and breathes and winks. Know it as Being and Non-Being, as the object of desire, higher than understanding, as the best of creatures. That which is flaming, subtler than the subtle, of which the worlds are set, and their inhabitants, that is the imperishable Brahman. It is life, speech and mind. That is the real. It is immortal.

Mundaka Upanishad, II, 2, 1–2

AS ONE and the same water is called by different names by different people, some calling it "water," some "vari," some "acqua," and some "pani" so the one Saccidananda – Existence-Bliss-Absolute – is invoked by some as God, by some as Allah, by some as Hari and by others as Brahman.

In a potter's shop there are vessels of different shapes and forms – pots, jars, dishes, plates etc. – but all made of the same clay. So God is one, but He is worshipped in different ages and climes under different names and forms.

Sayings of Shri Ramakrishna, No. 457

WE KNOW from Scripture that there is a Supreme Person whose nature is absolute bliss and goodness; who is fundamentally antagonistic to all evil; who is the cause of the origination, sustentation, and dissolution of the world; who differs in nature from all other beings, who is all-knowing, who by his mere thought and will accomplishes all his purposes; who is an ocean of kindness as it were for all who depend on him; who is all-merciful, who is immeasurably raised above all possibility of anyone being equal or superior to him, whose name is the *Highest Brahman*. And with equal certainty we know from Scripture that this Supreme Lord, when pleased by the faithful worship of his devotees, frees them from the influence of nescience which consists of *karma* accumulated in the infinite progress of time and hence hard to overcome, allows them to attain to that supreme bliss which consists in the direct intuition of His own true nature, and after that does not turn them back into the miseries of *samsara*. The text distinctly teaching this is: "One who behaves thus throughout life reaches the world of Brahman and does not return." And the Lord himself declared: "Having obtained me, great-souled men do not come into rebirth, the fleeting abode of misery, for they have reached the highest perfection." Nor indeed need we fear that the Supreme Lord when once having taken to himself the devotee whom he greatly loves will turn him back into the *samsara*. For he himself has said: "To the wise I am very dear and dear are they to me. Noble indeed are all these, but the wise I regard as my very self. For they, with soul devoted, seek me only as their highest goal. At the end of many births the wise go to me, thinking all is Vasudeva. Such great souled people are rarely met with."

RAMANUJA: *Shribhashya, IV, 4, 22*

NOTHING CAN be done except through the force of the Mother. When I speak of the Mother's force I do not speak of the force of Prakriti which carries in it things of the Ignorance but of the higher Force of the Divine that descends from above to transform the nature.

There is a force which accompanies the growth of the new consciousness and at once grows with it and helps it to come about and to perfect itself. This force is the Yoga-Shakti. It is here coiled up and asleep in all the centres of our inner being (Chakras) and is at the base of what is called in the Tantras the Kundalini Shakti. But it is also above us, above our head as the Divine Force – not there coiled up, involved, asleep, but awake, scient, potent, extended and wide; it is there waiting for manifestation and to this Force we have to open ourselves – to the power of the Mother. In the mind it manifests itself as a divine mind-force or a universal mind-force and it can do

everything that the personal mind cannot do; it is then the Yogic mind-force. When it manifests and acts in the vital or physical in the same way, it is there apparent as a Yogic life-force or a Yogic body-force. It can awake in all these forms, bursting outward and upwards, extending itself into wideness from below; or it can descend and become there a definite power for things; it can pour downwards into our body, working, establishing its reign, extending into wideness from above, link the lowest in us with the highest above us, release the individual into a cosmic universality or into absoluteness and transcendence.

Certainly, in a sense the descent of the higher powers is the Divine Mother's own descent – for it is she who comes down in them.

SHRI AUROBINDO: *On the Mother*, pp. 501–3

THERE IS one supreme Brahman diffused throughout the universe. It is worshipped by the worship of the universe, because everything exists in It. Even those who look to the fruit of action and are governed by their desires and by the worship of different gods and are addicted to various rituals go to and enter That.

He who sees everything in Brahman and who sees Brahman everywhere is undoubtedly known as a true Kaula, who has attained liberation while yet living.

Mahanirvana Tantra, X, 209f.

GOD IS not in the wood, not in the stone, not in the clay – God is in the feelings – feelings are God's cause.

Vriddha Canakya, 8, 12

THIS DIVINE Being, Saccidananda, is at once impersonal and personal: it is an Existence and the origin and foundation of all truths, forces, powers, existences, but it is also the one transcendent Conscious Being and the All-Person of whom all conscious beings are the selves and personalities; for He is their highest Self and the universal indwelling Presence. It is a necessity for the soul in the universe to know and to grow into this truth of itself, to become one with the Divine Being, to raise its nature to the Divine Nature, its existence to the Divine Existence, its consciousness into the Divine Consciousness, its delight of being into the Divine Delight of Being.

SHRI AUROBINDO: *The Life Divine, p. 789*

THE SUPREME Person is unsurpassed, and infinite joy in himself and by himself. He becomes the joy of another also, as his nature as joy is absolute and universal. When Brahman becomes the object of one's contemplation he (the meditator) becomes blissful. Thus the supreme Brahman is the ocean of infinite and unsurpassed excellence of attributes. He transcends all evil. The expanse of his glory is boundless. He abounds in surpassing condescension, maternal compassion, and supreme beauty. He is the principal entity. The individual self is subservient to him. If the seeker meditates on the Supreme with a full consciousness of this relationship and if the supreme Brahman so meditated upon becomes an object of supreme love to the devotee, then he himself effectuates the devotee's god-realization.

RAMANUJA: *Vedarthasangraha, No. 242f.*

THE WORK OF THE DIVINE

A S FROM a blazing fire, sparks by the thousands issue forth of like form, so from the Imperishable manifold beings are produced, and into it they also return.

Mundaka Upanishad, II, 1, 1

T HE WIND of God's grace is incessantly blowing. Lazy sailors on the sea of life do not take advantage of it. But the active and the strong always keep the sails of their minds unfurled to catch the favourable wind and thus reach their destination very soon.

Sayings of Shri Ramakrishna, No. 678

W HAT ARE the indications of God's advent into the human heart? As the glow of dawn heralds the rising sun, so unselfishness, purity and righteousness announce the advent of the Lord.

Sayings of Shri Ramakrishna, No. 937

I N A playful mood the Lord creates, preserves and reabsorbs the universe, but never gets attached to it. Abiding unperceived in the hearts of all living beings, he seems to enjoy the objects of the mind and of the five senses. But being the master of his Self he remains aloof from these objects. The doings of the Lord, revealed by his own word, no creature can comprehend any more than one can understand the performance of a magician. The power of the Lord is infinite; though he is the maker of this world, he remains forever beyond it.

Bhagavata Purana, I, 8

A LL THE worlds have I placed within my own self and my own self have I placed within all the worlds; all the gods have I placed within my own self and my own self have I placed within all the gods; all the Vedas have I placed within my own self, and my own self have I placed within the vital airs. For imperishable indeed are worlds, imperishable the gods, imperishable the Vedas, imperishable the vital airs, imperishable is the All: and whosoever knows this, passes from the perishable unto the imperishable, conquers recurrent death and attains the full measure of life.

Shatapatha Brahmana, VII, 11

THE ALL-LOVING Father, the Great Lord, does not force his presence on the soul not yet ripe to receive him. With infinite patience he waits and watches the struggle of the soul in *samsara* since the struggle is necessary for the full development of the faculties of the soul.

LOKACHARYA PILLAI: *Tattvatraya*

WHEN THE Lord, who is omnipotent, who knows all things and who is by His very nature full of love towards us, has accepted the responsibility (of saving us) there is nothing more remaining to be done by us here for it; let us therefore fix our souls in that boundless sea of supreme bliss and feel the satisfaction (of having attained our object) by becoming rich in rendering service to Him, poor though we may have been before. The person who has adopted surrender has from the time of its adoption nothing else to do for attaining its fruit. What had to be done was done by once performing self-surrender.

VEDANTA DESHIKA: *Rahasyatrayasara, XIII*

LOOKING AT your extremely varied creation
The mind that tries to understand it reels.
A painter without hands has drawn a picture

without colours onto a screen "emptiness".
It cannot be erased through washing
nor does the screen crumble away.
Suffering arises from looking at this body.
In that mirage dwells an extremely ferocious
  crocodile.
It has no real mouth, but it swallows all
who come to slake their thirst in the imaginary
  water.
Some call this world real, others unreal,
others assume that it is both real and unreal.
Tulsidas says: one who has found the true Self
leaves behind all these three errors.

TULSIDAS: *Keshav Kahi, 1, 4*

THE OMNIPOTENT Goddess, who is consciousness, who is truly the "I-consciousness", creates appearances of the world upon it like reflections in a mirror by her willpower, or the power of *maya* known as liberation.

All this world is reflected, like in a mirror, in consciousness. Seeing the reflections, one actually sees the mirror; likewise, experiencing the world appearance, one sees pure consciousness, God, the Self. Just as a mirror without reflecting a pot remains a mirror, so the highest consciousness remains itself, pure and undifferentiated, as soon as the world appearance created by thought activity is gone.

Do not conclude that there is no such thing as the world. Such thinking is imperfect and defective. Such a belief is impossible. One who tries to negate the whole world by the mere act of thought brings it to existence by that very act of negation. Just as a city reflected in a mirror is not a reality but exists as a reflection, so also this world is not a reality in itself but is consciousness all the same. This is self-evident. This is perfect knowledge.

There is no such thing as bondage or liberation. There is no such thing as the seeker and the means for seeking anything. Partless, Non-Dual, Conscious Energy, Tripura alone pervades everything. She is both knowledge and ignorance, bondage and liberation too. She is also the means for liberation. This is all one has to know.

Tripura Rahasya, Jnanakhanda, Ch. XXII (last section, condensed)

OUR RELATIONSHIP TO THE DIVINE

THIS IS the pathway through which the supreme Brahman is to be attained: by an accumulation of great merit the sins of the past gathered through all past lives are destroyed. Those whose sins are thus destroyed through great merit seek refuge at the feet of the Supreme Person. Such self-surrender generates an inclination towards him. Then they acquire knowledge of reality from the scriptures aided by the instruction of holy teachers. By steady effort they develop ever more such qualities of soul as control of mind, control of senses, austerity, purity, forgiveness, straightforwardness, discrimination as to what is to be feared and not feared, mercy and non-violence. They are devoted to the performance of their duties pertaining to their station in life and avoid actions prohibited; such conduct is considered worship of the Supreme Person. They offer their all and their very self at the lotus-like feet of the Supreme Person. Actuated by loving devotion to him, they constantly offer praise and obeisance, engage in remembrance of him, bow down before him in adoration perpetually, exert themselves always in the godward direction, always sing his glories, always listen to accounts of his perfections, speak constantly of those perfections, meditate upon him continuously, ceaselessly worship him and dedicate themselves once and for all to him.

The Supreme Person, who is overflowing with compassion, being pleased with such love, showers his grace on the aspirants, which destroys all their inner darkness. *Bhakti* develops in such devotees towards the Highest Person, a love that is valued for its own sake, uninterrupted, an absolute delight in itself. It is meditation that has taken on the character of the most vivid and immediate vision. Through such *bhakti* is the Supreme attained.

RAMANUJA: *Vedarthasangraha, No. 126*

THE FIRM and unshakable love of God which rises above all other ties of love and affection based upon an adequate knowledge and conviction of his great majesty is called *bhakti* (devotion). That alone is the means to *moksha* (liberation).

MADHVA: *Mahabharata Tatparya Nirnaya, I, 86*

WHEN WILL my eyes brim over with a flood of tears at the mention of your name, when will my mouth stammer with a breaking voice, and when will the hairs on my body stand up in a shower of ecstasy chanting your name?

Due to separation from Govinda a fraction of a moment appears like an aeon to me. My tears are flowing like the rain of the rainy season and the whole world is empty.

Whether he embraces me, who am devoted to his feet, or whether he crushes me and wounds my innermost being because he remains invisible. Whatever he does, the insatiable lover, he is the Lord of my life and no other.

CAITANYA: *Shikshashtaka, 6–8*

THE COMPANIONS of my birth, my hair, went white.
My concern for people's opinion has gone.
The body is wasted, the hands are trembling,
The light has gone out from the eyes.
The ear can no longer hear any word
And all senses have lost their strength.
The teeth are broken.
I cannot utter any understandable word.
Beauty has disappeared from my face.
Phlegm and bile are covering my throat.
I can call my son only with a movement of my hand.
Brothers, relations and, dearest of all, my wife
Are turning me out of my home.

As the moon has got a black mark, of which it cannot
    get rid
Thus I cannot rid myself of the attachment to what is
    "mine".
Tulsidas takes refuge to your powerful feet,
Which are able to overthrow greed.

TULSIDAS: *Mamata tu*

THE ABSOLUTE consciousness of its own free will is the cause of the manifestation of the universe. It is only when the ultimate consciousness comes into play that the universe opens its eyes and continues as existent, and when it withdraws its movement, the universe shuts its eyes. By the power of her own will, absolute consciousness unfolds the universe upon her screen. This universe is manifold because of the differentiation of mutually related objects and subjects.

The individual soul also in whom consciousness is contracted possesses the universe in a contracted form. The magnificent highest Shiva, desiring to manifest the universe which lies in him as identical with himself, flashes forth in the form of Sadasiva first as non-differentiated light. Then he unfolds himself in the totality of manifestations.

As the Lord is universe-bodied so the individual has the body of the entire universe in a contracted form. The ensouled being is identical with Shiva whose body is the universe, because light is his true nature. Knowledge of this truth alone constitutes liberation; want of this knowledge alone constitutes bondage.

KSHEMARAJA: *Pratyabhijnahridayam*

D O YOU aspire after Divine grace? Then propitiate the Mother, the Primal Energy (*shakti*). Yes, she is Mahamaya Herself. She is it Who has deluded the whole world, and is conjuring up the triple device of creation, maintenance, and dissolution. She has spread a veil of ignorance over all, and unless She unbars the gate, none can enter the "Inner Court". Let outside, we see only the external things, but the Eternal One, Saccidananda, remains ever beyond our ken.

The Divine Shakti has two aspects: Vidya [knowledge] and Avidya [ignorance]: Avidya deludes and is the mother of Kamini-Kanchana, "woman and gold"; and it binds. But Vidya is the source of devotion, kindness, knowledge and love, and it takes us towards God.

Sayings of Shri Ramakrishna, No. 441

THE SUPREME Brahman is characterized by truth, knowledge and bliss, and that is the only reality. The universe is perceived to be real, because it is superimposed upon Brahman, just as the blue colour is superimposed upon the sky. Whatever is negated by means of proof must needs be unreal. But that which is not so disproved must be real, if it is true at all times. The animate and the inanimate prove the existence of Brahman. When one says "I do not know Brahman" even that should be taken as proof of the existence of Brahman.

SHANKARA: *Sharirakabhashya, I, 1, 4*

IF I did not feel the presence of God within me, I see so much of misery and disappointment every day, that I would be a raving maniac and my destination would be the Hooghli.

MAHATMA GANDHI: *Young India, 6 Aug. 1925*

I AM endeavouring to see God through service of humanity, for I know that God is neither in heaven, nor down below, but in every one.

MAHATMA GANDHI: *Young India, 4 Aug. 1927*

MINE MUST be a state of complete resignation to the Divine Will. And if I had the impertinence openly to declare my wish to live 125 years I must have the humility under changed circumstances openly to shed that wish. I have done no more, no less. This has not been done in a spirit of depression, the more apt term perhaps is helplessness. In that state I invoke the aid of the all-embracing Power to take me away from this "vale of tears" rather than make me a helpless witness of the butchery by man become savage. Yet I cry "Not my will, but Thine alone shall prevail." If He wants me, He will keep me here on this earth, yet a while.

TENDULKAR: *Mahatma, VIII, 196*

I BELIEVE in absolute oneness of God and therefore also of humanity. What though we have many bodies? We have but one soul.

MAHATMA GANDHI: *Young India, 25 Sept. 1924*

I BELIEVE in advaita. I believe in the essential unity of man and for that matter of all that lives.

MAHATMA GANDHI: *Young India, 4 Dec. 1924*

THE DIVINE Will is not an alien Power or Presence, it is intimate to us and we ourselves are part of it, for it is our own highest Self that possesses and supports it. The Divine Will is superconscious to us because it is in its essence supra-mental, and it knows all, because it is all.

SHRI AUROBINDO: *The Synthesis of Yoga*, p. 55

Our Relationship to the Divine ↝ 37

JUST AS you seek the udder of the cow for the milk it gives, seek the Lord and His Glory only in nature. As a matter of fact, Nature is useful only when it adds to the wonder and awe that it is able to provoke and sustain. Everything is an image of the Lord. Krishna revelled in seeing His own images in the Mani Mantapa of His house, when He was a child. Just as the Lord is pleased when He sees Himself in His manifestations called Nature. That is why there is such a joy welling up in all when they hear the story of the Lord and how He calls all to Himself. It is the call of the Bimba [image] for the Pratibimba [original], to merge in it. So all are entitled for the merging, all finally have to attain it. Otherwise there is no meaning for the yearning to become greater and greater.

Sathya Sai Speaks, III, 170

EXPERIENCE OF the Divine must be sought in the company of good people. It is an illusion to imagine that you can see God in some temple or shrine or in some kind of meditation. Only in the Divine manifesting in a human form can you experience the Divine. If one cannot experience the Divine in a living human being, how can one experience it in an inanimate stone? It is only when one perceives with love that one realises one's true nature.

Sathya Sai Speaks, XI, 61

THE NAME OF THE DIVINE

T HE SINGING of Shri Krishna's name is extremely victorious: it cleanses the mirror of the mind, it extinguishes the forest fire of *samsara*, it is the gift of moonshine for the lotus of the heart, it is the power of wisdom, it makes the ocean of joy of divine service surge, it makes us taste holy passion in every syllable, it is a soothing bath for all Selves.

You have revealed your many names in many ways and you have placed into these names your entire being. There is no restriction for singing these names. So great, O Lord, is your grace, but my fate in this birth is quite horrible, because there has not arisen in me an overpowering love for your name.

CAITANYA: *Shikshashtaka, 1 and 2*

I N THE *Kaliyuga* the singing of the name is the great *sadhana*. Through *samkirtana* the sin of the world is destroyed, the heart is purified and practice of all kinds of *bhakti* is initiated.

Caitanya Caritamrita, II, 9; III, 20

A PRAYER

I HAVE fallen so lowly:
I do not even have one bit of desire for you!
Powerful Maya has fettered me
in the guise of property, money and a fair wife.
I see it, I hear it, I know it,
but I still cannot get away from it.
With my own ears I have perceived: it was said
you are the salvation of those who have fallen very
    low.
I want to get into the boat of deliverance,
but I am unable to pay the fare to the boatman.
I do not ask anything new from you,
you have always been gracious towards the poor.
Incline with favour upon Sur,
Lord, King of Braja.

SURDAS: *Kijai prabhu*

LIFE AND DEATH

LIFE IS only relatively real; until death, it appears to be real, that is all. For the procession of the bride and groom, the father of the bride had brought an elephant, or rather the model of an elephant, correct to the minutest detail. The model was taken by all who saw it to be alive. Then, while all were admiring the wonderful work of art and arguing that it was alive, it exploded, shooting forth lovely little stars and snakes of light that gleamed through the sky. It was filled with fireworks, and when it was lit, the entire stock filling the inside emerged, with a burst of noise and a brilliant riot of light and colour.

Man is like that elephant, true, until the explosion. Before the explosion happens, man must realise himself. The fireworks are Kama (lust), Krodha (anger), Moha (delusion), Mada (intoxication) etc. and they now fill this artificial animal, useful only for the show. Man is saved from such calamity by Vedanta. Vedanta is like the roar of the lion, it gives courage and enterprise, it makes man a hero.

Sathya Sai Speaks, III, 172

IF THERE were no birth, no old age, and no death, if there were no fear of separation from a loved one, and if everything were not transient – who would not enjoy to live on earth?

Subhashitarnava, 35

THE WISE do not grieve for the dead or the living. Never was there a time when I was not, nor you, nor these others, nor will there ever be a time when we shall cease to be. As the soul passes in this body through childhood, youth and old age, even so it is taking on another body. The sage is not perplexed by this.

Bhagavadgita, II, 11–13

KARMA AND REBIRTH

RISE UP to the heavens or move to the ends of the world, plunge into the deep sea or stay where you are: the consequences of works, that bring fortune and misfortune to people, accumulated in previous lives, will follow you like a shadow.

Sahityadarpana, 3, 21

LIKE INDIGESTIBLE food in the belly, an evil deed is its own punishment – if not experienced in one's own life, it will hurt sons or grandsons.

Mahabharata, I, 75

THE REWARD for a good deed performed in this world will be enjoyed in the next world; when one waters the roots of trees fruits form at their branches.

Subhashitarnava, 271

GRASS WAS I, a shrub, a worm, a tree,
All kinds of beast, bird, snake,
Stone, man, and demon.
Born within these many forms of life,
I have grown weary, O great Lord!
But, seeing your golden pair of feet today,
I have gained release.

You know no change
You create and protect and destroy all worlds.
You give rich grace and release.
You are more subtle than sweet fragrance.
You are far as well as near,
And you cut through the chain of births – you
    mighty One!

MANIKKA VACAKAR: *Tiruvacakam, I, 26–48*

FATE

THE SUCCESS of one's actions rests equally on destiny and personal effort. Destiny is the fruit of efforts made in a previous life. As a chariot cannot move on one wheel alone, so without personal effort destiny alone accomplishes nothing.

Yajnavalkyasmriti, I, 349. 353

NOBLE BIRTH, health, beauty, prosperity, and objects of enjoyment are all won through destiny. The poor, although they may not want them, have many children, while the rich, who desire them, have none. Wonderful is the course of destiny! According to the destiny under which one is born one is overtaken by evils such as disease, fire, water, weapons, hunger, poison, fever, death, and falling from high places. One who is free from sin suffers calamities, while sinners are living happily. A rich man dies young and a poor fellow drags on his existence, weighed down by decrepitude, for a hundred years. All this is the work of destiny.

Mahabharata, XII, 28

WHAT IS not meant to be will never be; what is meant to be will happen by itself. If fate has so ordained, even that will disappear what you already hold in your hand.

Pancatantra, III

A POOR carp slid out from the fisher's hand, who had caught him, but fell back into the net. He escaped from the net, only to be swallowed by a heron. If fate is against you, how can you escape misfortune?

Pancatantra, II

WHAT IS going to be will fall into your hand, even if it is beyond the seas; what is not going to be will escape you, even if it is already lying on the palm of your hand.

Subhashitarnava, 36

THERE IS no friend like knowledge, no enemy like disease, no love like that to one's child, no power greater than fate.

Canakya, 75

A MAN whose hour has not yet come does not die although transfixed by a hundred arrows; a man whose hour has come does not remain alive if just touched by the tip of a blade of grass.

Mahabharata, XIII, 149

TIME

TIME OF its own power cooks all beings within itself. No one, however, knows that in which Time itself is being cooked.

Mahabharata, XII, 249

ALL THE jewels in the world cannot buy a single moment of our life; to waste such a moment is great folly.

Subhashitarnava, 69

TIME BRINGS forth creatures and takes them away; time also takes to rest the time that takes away the creatures.

Mahabharata, III, 57

HUMAN NATURE

MAN IS not complete; he is yet to be. In what he *is* he is small; and if we could conceive him stopping there for eternity we should have an idea of the most awful hell that man can imagine. In his *to be* he is infinite, there is his heaven, his deliverance. His *is* is occupied every moment with what it can get and have done with; his *to be* is hungering for something which is more than can be got, which he never can lose because he never has possessed.

RABINDRANATH TAGORE: *Sadhana (VIII)*, p. 153

THERE IS nothing final or eternal about states or nations which wax and wane. But the humblest individual has the spark of spirit in him, which the mightiest empire cannot crush. Rooted in one life, we are all fragments of the divine, sons of immortality.

S. RADHAKRISHNAN: *Religion and Society*, p. 66

A MAN'S heart is always good at the core. It may get rusted on the outside on account of various internal factors but its goodness remains always the same, whatever the outward appearance. It is like the head of a cabbage whose outer layer may be bad but the inside layers retain their freshness.

VINOBA BHAVE: *quoted by Suresh Ram, Vinoba and His Mission, p. 348*

THERE IS a very deep river called hope: wishes are its waters, desires form its waves, that move the river, passions are the crocodiles in it, considerations are the birds that move to and fro; firmness is the tree at the banks, whom the river undermines, ignorance is the vortex that makes crossing difficult, the mountains of cares are the high banks. May the great sages who have renounced everything and who live in meditation enjoy themselves after having crossed this river with pure hearts.

Bhartrihari, II, 45

HAPPINESS AND ITS LIMITS

FTER EVERY happiness comes misery; they may be far apart or near. The more advanced the soul, the more quickly does one follow the other. What we want is neither happiness nor misery. Both make us forget our true nature; both are chains, one iron, another gold; behind both is the Atman, who knows neither happiness nor misery. These are states and states must ever change; but the nature of the soul is bliss, peace, unchanging. We have not to get it, we have it; only wash away the dross and see it.

SWAMI VIVEKANANDA: *Inspired Talks, 25 June 1895*

HESE SIX are always unhappy: one who is envious, one who has too soft a heart, one who is discontent, one who is angry, one who is always afraid of something, and one who lives on other people's handouts.

Mahabharata, V, 183

THERE IS no possibility of ever having pleasure without pain, good without evil, for living itself is just the lost equilibrium. What we want is freedom, not life, nor pleaure, nor good. Creation is infinite, without beginning and without end, the ever moving ripple in an infinite lake. There are yet unreached depths and others where the equilibrium has been regained but the ripple is always progressing, the struggle to regain the balance is eternal. Life and death are only different names for the same fact, the two sides of one coin.

SWAMI VIVEKANANDA: *Inspired Talks, 25 June, 1895*

MAN'S ABIDING happiness is not in getting anything but in giving himself up to what is greater than himself, to ideas which are larger than his individual life, the idea of his country, of humanity, of God. They make it easier for him to part with all he has, not excepting his life. His existence is miserable and sordid till he finds some great idea which can truly claim his all, which can release him from all attachment to his belongings.

RABINDRANATH TAGORE: *Sadhana (VIII), p. 152*

LOVE

LOVE AND suffering go together. No one who really loves can escape suffering. The more you love, the more you suffer.

S. RADHAKRISHNAN: *East and West in Religion*, *p. 110*

MAN IS born through love, he grows through love, he thirsts for it in his last moments and feels supremely comforted when he gets it. If, therefore, his entire life, in its beginning, the middle and the end, depends upon love, if that is for him the source of his greatest delight, why would he not feel prompted to give his poorer brethren a due share of what he has in land and wealth?

VINOBA BHAVE: *quoted by Suresh Ram, Vinoba and His Mission, p. 407*

THERE IS no disease like love, no enemy like error, no fire like anger, and no joy like knowledge.

Vriddha Canakya, 5, 12

TRANSIENCE

ALL PROVISIONS will come to an end one day, rising will end with falling, associations will end with separations, and life will end with death.

Mahabharata, XII, 27

JOY IS followed by sorrows and sorrows are followed by joy: one is neither always joyful nor always sorrowful.

Mahabharata, III, 247

ANIMALS LIVE upon animals, the stronger upon the weaker. Mongoose devour mice; cats devour mongoose; dogs devour cats; dogs again are devoured by spotted leopards. All things are devoured by the Destroyer, when he comes. This universe, made up of things mobile and immobile, is food for living creatures. This has been ordained by the gods. The wise are not dismayed by this.

Mahabharata, XII, 15

N O MAN knows sorrow as long as he is in possession of his pleasant home, family and wealth; but why should he be sorrowful upon their disappearance, knowing them as a short-lived enchantment and accompaniment?

What pleasure or pain can one derive, either from the grandeur or destruction of his castle in the air, and what cause of joy can he have in his ignorant children, or of sorrow upon their death?

What joy is there in the increase of our wealth or family, seeing them as the increasing mirage of water which can never satisfy the thirsty?

Care increases with the increase of wealth and family; and there is no true happiness in the increase of worldly possessions and affections.

Yogavasishta Ramayana, IV, 46

DESIRE

IN THE human heart grows a wonderful tree, called desire. It is born of the seed called error. Wrath and pride constitute its large trunk. The wish for action is the watering basin at its foot. Ignorance is the root of that tree, and heedlessness is the water that gives it sustenance. Envy constitutes its leaves. The evil acts of past lives supply it with vigour. Loss of judgement and anxiety are its twigs, grief forms its large branches, and fear is its sprout. Thirst for pleasure forms the creepers that cling on it. Greedy fellows, bound in chains of iron, sitting round that fruit-yielding tree, pay their homage to it in expectation of obtaining its fruit. Those who shed these chains and cut down that tree cast off both sorrow and joy and succeed in attaining the ends of both. The foolish who nourish that tree by indulging their senses are destroyed by those very enjoyments like patients who consume poisonous medicine. A skilled person tears up and cuts through the deep root of the tree with the sword of wisdom.

Mahabharata, XII, 240

RULES TO LIVE BY

ESSENTIALS

GOD IS the primary cause of all true knowledge and of everything known by its means.

God is All-truth, All-knowledge, All-beatitude, Incorporal, Almighty, Just, Merciful, Unbegotten, Infinite, Unchangeable, Without a beginning, Incomparable, the Support and the Lord of all, All-pervading, Omniscient, Imperishable, Immortal, Exempt from fear, Eternal, Holy and the cause of the universe. To him alone worship is due.

The Vedas are the books of true knowledge and it is the paramount duty of every Arya to read or hear them read, to teach and read them to others.

An Arya should always be ready to accept truth and to renounce untruth.

All actions must conform to virtue, that is, should be performed after a thorough consideration of right and wrong.

The primary object of the Samaj is to benefit the whole world, viz. by improving the physical, spiritual, and social condition of mankind.

All ought to be treated with love and justice and with due regard to their merits.

Ignorance must be dispelled and knowledge diffused.

No one should be contented with his own good alone, but everyone should regard his or her prosperity as included in that of others.

In matters which affect the general social well-being of our race none should allow his or her individuality to interfere with the general good, but in strictly personal affairs, everyone may act with freedom.

The Ten Principles of the Arya Samaj

I WILL give you a talisman. Whenever you are in doubt, or when the self becomes too much with you, apply the following test: Recall the face of the poorest and the weakest man whom you may have seen and ask yourself if the step that you contemplate is going to be of any use to *him*. Will he gain anything by it? Will it restore him to a control over his own life and destiny? In other words, will it lead to Swaraj (self-rule) for the hungry and spiritually starving millions? Then you will find your doubts and your self melting away.

TENDULKAR: *Mahatma, VIII, 288*

MAKE FOUR resolutions about your life. Purity: Desist from wicked thoughts, bad habits, low activities, that weaken your self-respect. Service: Serve others, for they are the reflections of the same Entity of which you are yourself a reflection. No one of you has any authenticity, except with reference to the One Original. Mutuality: Feel always kinship with all creation. See the same current flowing through all the objects in the universe. Truth: Do not deceive yourself or others, by distorting your experience.

Sathya Sai Speaks, II, 213f.

LET YOUR mother be a god to you. Let your father be a god to you. Let your teacher be a god to you. Let your guest be a god to you. Let only these works be done by you that are free from blemishes. Only deeds that are good are to be performed by you.

Taittiriya Upanishad, I, XI, 1–2

THERE IS no treasure greater than charity, no wealth greater than contentment, no jewel more precious than good character and no object more desirable than health.

Pancatantra, II

HEALTH, FREEDOM from debts, living in one's own home-country, association with good people, a secure income and a safe dwelling are the six great fortunes of men.

Mahabharata, V, 183

BY MEANS of the one (mind) discern between the two (righteousness and unrighteousness), with the help of the four (good words, gifts, dissent among associates, and force) subdue the three (friends, neutrals and enemies), conquer the five (senses), become acquainted with the six (alliance, war, campaign, truce, division of armies and refuge with a more powerful one), avoid the seven (women, dice, hunting, drink, insult through words, assault, appropriation of others' property) and then live happily.

Mahabharata, V, 33

ONE SHOULD not have one's dwelling where these four are missing: a money lender, a physician, a priest versed in the scriptures, and a river with good water.

Markandeya Purana, 34

THESE SIX one should never give up: truthfulness, generosity, good humour, friendliness, forgiveness and contentment.

Mahabharata, V, 33

A TIGER without a forest will be killed, a forest without a tiger will be cut down: thus the tiger protects the forest and the forest saves the tiger.

Mahabharata, V, 29

ONE OUGHT not to covet another man's wife or possessions, one ought not speak ill of another, one ought not to deride a teacher and one ought not constantly to change one's domicile.

Canakya, 30

THE BODY is like a chariot, the mind like a charioteer, the senses like horses: someone prudently driving it enjoys a pleasant ride like the owner of a coach with his shining well-trained horses.

Mahabharata, III, 202

NO PERSON should regard herself inferior; because there is no happiness for one who regards oneself low.

Mahabharata, XII, 129

DO NOT spend a day in a place where you cannot acquire knowledge, where you cannot earn money, and where you do not feel comfortable.

Subhashitarnava, 196

DO TODAY what has to be done tomorrow; do this morning what has to be done this evening; death does not wait for you to complete your task.

Mahabharata, XII, 169

IF YOU want to live happily cultivate contentment and self-control: happiness is founded on contentment, discontent is the root of suffering.

Manusmriti, IV, 12

THE RELATION between the body and the mind is so intimate that, if either of them got out of order, the whole system would suffer. Hence it follows, that a pure character is the foundation of health in the real sense of the term, and we may say that all evil thoughts and evil passions are but different forms of disease.

MAHATMA GANDHI: *A Guide to Health*, p. 3

DHARMA

RIGHTEOUSNESS (*DHARMA*) was declared by Brahman for the advancement and growth of all creatures. Therefore that which leads to advancement and growth is righteousness. Righteousness was declared for restraining creatures from injuring one another. Therefore that is righteousness which prevents injury to creatures. Righteousness is so called, because it upholds all creatures. In fact, all creatures are upheld by righteousness. Therefore that is righteousness which is capable of upholding all creatures.

Mahabharata, XII, 110

DO NOT do to another what you do not like to be done to yourself; that is the gist of the law – all other laws are variable.

Mahabharata, V, 39

YOU HAVE come into this world to do business and
    make a profit,
but you have gambled away your stock.
You have not even reached the outskirts of the City
    of Love.
As you have come, so you shall leave.
Listen my companion! Listen my friend!
What have you done in this life?
You have taken up a load of stones on your head!
Who will lift it from you further down the road?
Your friend is standing on the shore
and you have no mind to meet him.
You are sitting in a shipwrecked boat.
You fool! You will be drowning!
Kabirdas who observes all this says:
In the end, who is your helper?
Alone did you go forth, and you will eat your own
    deeds.

KABIR: *Re dil*

PERFORM YOUR duties in an unselfish spirit. Always try to perform your duties without desiring any result. All without exception perform work. Even to chant the name and glories of God is work as is the meditation of the non-dualist on "I am He": Breathing is also an activity. There is no way of renouncing work altogether. So do your work, but surrender the results to God.

You may try to increase your income, but in an honest way. The goal of life is not the earning of money but the service of God. Money is not harmful if it is devoted to the service of God.

One doesn't have to do one's duty after the attainment of God, nor does one feel like doing it then. As you advance nearer and nearer to God, He will reduce your activities little by little.

The Gospel of Ramakrishna, pp. 41f.

YOU BROUGHT much money with you when you
    entered this city.
Tie it up in your garment to protect it from thieves!
In the business for which you had come, you hardly
    made any profit.
This is a matter of great concern.
You have fallen into the sleep of falsehood.
Unthinkingly you have lost all your money; you
    make all sad.
Krishnadas says: go home!
When Krishna comes fall at his feet and find rest!

KRISHNADAS: *Musaphir Sota hai*

TO ACTION alone you have a right, never to its fruit; let not the
fruits of action be your motive nor let there be in you
attachment to inaction. Do your work, abandoning
attachment, with an even mind in success and failure.

Bhagavadgita, II, 47–8

TRUST

WE SHOULD not trust someone, who does not trust us; but we should not have absolute trust in one who trusts us, either. We should always endeavour to make others trust us, but we should never fully trust others.

Mahabharata, XII, 136

EVEN A weak enemy should not be taken lightly; even a small fire can burn down an entire forest, once it has established itself.

Mahabharata, IV, 28

NON-VIOLENCE

NON-VIOLENCE is an active force of the highest order. It is soul force or the power of Godhead within us. Imperfect man cannot grasp the whole of that Essence – he would not be able to bear its full blaze, but even an infinitesimal fraction of it, when it becomes active within us, can work wonders.

MAHATMA GANDHI: *Harijan, 12 Nov. 1932*

NON-VIOLENCE is common to all religions, but it has found the highest expression and application in Hinduism. (I do not regard Jainism or Buddhism as separate from Hinduism.) Hinduism believes in the oneness not of merely all human life, but in the oneness of all that lives. Its worship of the cow is, in my opinion, its unique contribution to the evolution of humanitarianism. It is a practical application of the belief in the oneness and, therefore, sacredness of all life. The great belief in transmigration is a direct consequence of that belief.

MAHATMA GANDHI: *Harijan, 27 Apr. 1927*

AHIMSA IS not the goal. Truth is the goal. But we have no means of realizing truth in human relationships except through the practice of *ahimsa* (non-violence). A steadfast pursuit of *ahimsa* is inevitably bound to truth – not so violence. That is why I swear by *ahimsa*. Truth came naturally to me. *Ahimsa* I acquired after a struggle.

MAHATMA GANDHI: *Harijan, 23 June 1946*

THE PATH of true non-violence requires much more courage than violence.

MAHATMA GANDHI: *Harijan, 4 Aug. 1946*

NON-VIOLENCE is the greatest force at the disposal of mankind. It is mightier than the mightiest weapon of destruction devised by the ingenuity of man. Destruction is not the law of the humans. Man lives freely by his readiness to die, if need be, at the hands of his brother, never by killing him. Every murder or other injury, no matter for what cause, committed or inflicted on another is a crime against humanity.

MAHATMA GANDHI: *Harijan, 12 Nov. 1938*

ALL SOCIETY is held together by non-violence, even as the earth is held in her position by gravitation. But when the law of gravitation was discovered, the discovery yielded results of which our ancestors had no knowledge. Even so, when society is deliberately constructed in accordance with the law of non-violence, its structure will be different in material particulars from what it is today.

MAHATMA GANDHI: *Harijan, 11 Feb. 1939*

MY CREED of non-violence is an extremely active force. It has no room for cowardice or even weakness. There is hope for a violent man to be some day non-violent, but there is none for a coward.

MAHATMA GANDHI: *Young India, 16 June 1927*

I DO BELIEVE that, where there is only a choice between cowardice and violence, I would advise violence. But I believe that non-violence is infinitely superior to violence, forgiveness is more manly than punishment. Forgiveness adorns the soldier.

MAHATMA GANDHI: *Young India, 11 Aug. 1920*

I AM MORE concerned in preventing the brutalization of human nature than in the prevention of the sufferings of my own people. I know that people who voluntarily undergo a course of suffering raise themselves and the whole of humanity. If we are all sons of the same God and partake of the same divine essence, we must partake of the sin of every person whether he belongs to us or to another race.

MAHATMA GANDHI: *Young India, 29 Oct. 1931*

A VOTARY of *ahimsa* cannot subscribe to the utilitarian formula of the greatest good of the greatest number. He will strive for the greatest good of all and die in the attempt to realize the ideal. He will therefore be willing to die so that the others may live.

MAHATMA GANDHI: *Young India, 9 Dec. 1926*

RESPECT FOR EVERYTHING

THERE IS a consciousness in things, a life which is not the life and consciousness of man and animal which we know, but still secret and real. That is why we must have a respect for physical things and use them rightly, not misuse and waste, ill-treat or handle them with a careless roughness. This feeling of all being consciousness – and not the mind only – awakes out of its obscurity and becomes aware of the One in all things, the Divine everywhere.

SHRI AUROBINDO: *On Himself, 469*

THE MIDDLE PATH

THE GODDESS of Fortune is afraid of one who is too honest, too generous, too heroic, too pious and one who considers himself smart. She does not dwell with those who are too virtuous nor with those who are too wicked – like a mad cow the blind goddess makes halt wherever.

Mahabharata, V, 39

ONE SHOULD not be too straight. Go and look at a forest: the straight trees are cut down whereas the crooked are left standing.

Vriddha Canakya, 7, 12

A PRINCE, fire, a teacher and a woman mean disaster if one comes too close; too far away they are of no use – one has to deal with them from an appropriate distance.

Vriddha Canakya, 14, 11

FRIENDSHIP

MAKE FRIENDSHIP with someone who is shrewd and upright; beware of someone shrewd and false. Have pity for one who is foolish and upright; but avoid one who is foolish and false.

Pancatantra, II

A BAD friend is like an earthen jar: it breaks easily and is impossible to repair. A good friend is like a vessel made of gold: it is hard to break and easy to mend.

Pancatantra, II

IT IS better to lose one's life than to lose one's friends; life returns after it ends, friendship does not return.

Pancatantra, II

FRIENDSHIP IS made up of these six things: give and take, talk and listen, entertain and be entertained. No friendship arises without some friendly act; even the gods require gifts for their grace. Friendship ceases with the cessation of gifts; the calf leaves the mother-cow who has gone dry.

Pancatantra, II

FRIENDS TAKE on the guise of foes and foes assume the guise of friends. There is no such thing as a permanent foe or friend. It is force of circumstance that creates foes and friends. One who regards his own interests safe as long as another person lives and thinks them endangered when the other person will cease to live, takes that other person for a friend and considers him so, as long as those interests of his are not diminished. There is no condition that deserves permanently the name of friendship or hostility. Both friendship and enmity arise from considerations of interest and gain. Friendship becomes changed into enmity in the course of time. A foe also can become a friend. Self-interest is very powerful.

Mahabharata, XII, 136

ONE SHOULD entertain neither friendship nor enmity towards an evil person: a piece of coal, when it is hot burns the hand, when it is cold blackens it.

Hitopadesha, I

THE SELF

THE NATURE OF THE SELF

JUST AS a person casts off worn-out garments and puts on others that are new, even so the embodied soul casts off worn-out bodies and takes on others that are new. Weapons do not cleave the Self, fire does not burn the Self, waters do not drench the Self, winds do not parch the Self. The Self is eternal, all-pervading, unchanging and immovable. The Self is the same forever: unmanifest, unthinkable, still.

Bhagavadgita, II, 22–5

THE SELF is below, the Self is above, the Self is to the west, the Self is to the east, the Self is to the south, the Self is to the north. The Self, indeed is this whole universe.

Chandogya Upanishad, VII, XV, 1

THE SELF which is free from evil, from aging, from death, from sorrow, from hunger, from thirst, whose desire is the Real, whose conception is the Real – that should be searched out, and one should strive to understand it. One obtains all worlds and all desires if one has found out and understands that Self.

Chandogya Upanishad, VIII, VII, 1

THE ONE who dwells in all things, yet is other than all things, whom all things do not know, whose body all things are, who controls all things from within – That is your Self, the Inner Controller, the Immortal. That is the unseen Seer, the unheard Hearer, the unthought Thinker, the ununderstood Understander. Other than That there is no seer. Other than That there is no hearer. Other than That there is no thinker. Other than That there is no understander. That is Your Self, the Inner Controller, the Immortal.

Brihadaranyaka Upanishad, III, VII, 15.23

VERILY, THIS self is Brahman, made of knowledge, of mind, of breath, of seeing, of hearing, of earth, of water, of wind, of space, of energy and non-energy, of desire and non-desire, of anger and non-anger, of virtuousness and non-virtuousness. It is made of everything.

Brihadaranyaka Upanishad, IV, IV, 5

THE SOUL is without beginning and without end. Immersed in one's Soul one should move and act without giving way to wrath, without giving in to joy, and always free from envy. Cutting the knots in one's heart one should live happily without giving way to grief and with one's doubts dispelled.

Mahabharata, XII, 149

IN ME, the unlimited ocean, the vessel of the universe moves about, impelled by the wind of its own nature. I am not moved by it.

In me, the unlimited ocean, the wave of the universe rises or vanishes according to its own nature. I am neither increasing nor decreasing by it.

In me, the unlimited ocean, the universe of imagination develops. I am tranquil and formless. In this alone I dwell.

The Self is not in the object and the object is not in That which is infinite and stainless. It is free from attachment and desire and is still. In this alone do I dwell.

I am pure Consciousness. The world is like a magic show. How should there be in me any notion of attractiveness or repulsiveness?

Ashtavakra Samhita, VII

THIS BODY, verily is mortal. It has been appropriated by death. But it is the standing-ground of that bodiless, deathless Self. One who is in a body has been appropriated by pleasure and pain. There is no freedom from pleasure and pain for one who is in a body. One who is bodiless, is untouched by pleasure and pain.

Chandogya Upanishad, VIII, VII, 1ff.

ACCORDING AS one acts, according as one conducts oneself, so does one become. The doer of good becomes good. The doer of evil becomes evil. One becomes virtuous by virtuous action, bad by bad action.

As is one's desire so is one's resolve, such an action one performs; what action one performs, that one procures for oneself. One who is without desire, who is freed from desire, whose desire is satisfied does not pass on to another birth. Being Brahman he enters into Brahman.

One who has found and has awakened the Self that has entered this composite body, that one is the maker of everything, the creator of all; the world is that one's; that one is the world itself.

In the cave of the heart lies the Ruler of all, the Lord of all, the King of all. That one does not become greater by good action nor less by bad action. That is the Lord of all, the Overlord of beings, the Protector of beings.

Brihadaranyaka Upanishad, IV, 5.13.22

THERE IS nothing final, or eternal about states or nations which wax and wane. But the humblest individual has the spark of spirit in him which the mightiest empire cannot crush. Rooted in one life, we are all fragments of the divine, sons of immortality.

S. RADHAKRISHNAN: *Religion and Society, p. 66*

THE HUMAN self is a temporary unstable organization oscillating between the matter which offers the possibility of existence and the spirit who moulds it into significant being. It strives after integration. Integrated lives are the sacred ones. They possess the joy unspeakable, the peace that surpasseth understanding. The new society will be built by those who have deepened their personalities and integrated their lives. The imperfect social order is a challenge to those who have achieved inner strength and integrity.

S. RADHAKRISHNAN: *My Search for Truth, pp. 31f.*

THERE CANNOT be any conflict between body, mind and soul. The harmony of the different sides of our nature is the condition of peace and their mutual understanding the means of perfection. The suppression of any other side mars self-fulfilment. Asceticism is an excess indulged in by those who exaggerate the transcendent aspect of reality. The mystic does not regard any antithesis between the secular and the sacred. Nothing is to be rejected, everything is to be raised.

S. RADHAKRISHNAN: *Idealist View of Life*, p. 115

HUMAN INDIVIDUALS are not unchanging substrata of change with accidental qualities and related to one another externally, but are elements in an interrelated system. They are centers of experience or processes of becoming through a creative synthesis of their relations. They possess a certain relative independency though the general nature of the system conditions them all. Instead of being a self-contained individual each empirical self is the expression or focusing of something beyond itself. The real whole or individual is that which includes persons and their environments and these exist in themselves by a process of abstraction.

S. RADHAKRISHNAN: *Idealist View of Life*, p. 272

THERE IS, no doubt, something in human existence which is specially connected with religion and its goal. It is "Reality". But "Reality" is no part of human existence, rather human existence can be (so to say) called a part of that "Reality". The "Reality" is an endless ocean in which human beings are like waves. That "Reality" is named *atma* [self] in Hindu scriptures. It is All-pervading and Omnipresent.

As regards the connection between the *atma*, the Real Self, and the individual limited self, it is stated in the Hindu scriptures that "to rise above names and forms and to give up the limitations of body, mind and intellect, is to become All Knowledge, All Bliss and All Energy". For example, the bubbles and the waves of the river, on giving up their names and forms, are in reality pure water which is sweet, crystal clear, all pervading and interpenetrating.

SWAMI RAMA TIRTHA: *In Woods of God-Realization*, V, 3

CONSCIOUSNESS IS the holy well, wherein all the gods, the scriptures and the sacred rituals become one. A bath in that well makes one immortal.

SHANKARA: *Upadeshasahasri, XIV, 40*

FREEING AND FINDING THE SELF

ONE SHOULD lift up oneself by oneself; let no one degrade one's self; for the Self alone is the friend of the self, and the Self alone is the enemy of the self. To the one who has conquered the self by the Self, the Self is a friend, but to the one who is not at home in the Self, this very Self will act like an enemy. When one has conquered one's self and has attained to the calm of self-mastery, this Supreme Self abides in oneself ever steady: one is at peace in cold and heat, in pleasure and pain, in honour and dishonour.

Bhagavadgita, VI, 5–7

ONE WHO considers oneself free is free indeed and one who considers oneself bound remains bound. "As one thinks, so one becomes", is a popular saying in this world which is very true.

Ashtavakra Samhita, I, 20

I F YOU aspire after liberation, shun the objects of the senses like poison, and seek forgiveness, sincerity, kindness, contentment and truth as nectar. You are neither earth, nor water, nor fire, nor air, nor ether. In order to gain liberation, know the Self as witness of all these and pure consciousness. Virtue and vice, pleasure and pain are properties of the mind, not of you. You are neither doer nor enjoyer; you are ever free.

Ashtavakra Samhita, I, 2.3.6

T HE SELF, hidden in all beings, does not reveal itself to everyone. It is seen by those of subtle and concentrated mind. Having realized that which is without sound, without touch, formless, imperishable, and also without taste and smell, eternal, without beginning or end, beyond all manifestation – one is liberated from death. When all desires that dwell in the heart are destroyed, when all the knots of the heart are rent asunder, then a mortal becomes immortal and here in this very body attains the infinite.

Katha Upanishad, III, 12; IV, 14–15

By DISCERNING that which is soundless, touchless, formless, imperishable, tasteless, constant, odourless, without beginning, without end, higher than the great, stable – one is liberated from the mouth of death.

Katha Upanishad, III, 15

THIS ATMAN is not to be obtained by instruction, nor by intellect, nor by much learning. It is to be obtained only by the one whom it chooses, to such a one the *atman* reveals its own being. This *atman* is not to be obtained by one devoid of fortitude, nor through heedlessness, nor through a false notion of austerity. But one who strives by these means, provided one knows, into this Brahman-abode this *atman* enters.

Mundaka Upanishad, III, 2, 3–4

OUR BEST work is done, our greatest influence is exerted, when we are without the thought of self. All great geniuses know this. Let us open ourselves to the one Divine Actor and let Him act, and do nothing ourselves. Be perfectly resigned, perfectly unconcerned; then alone can you do any true work.

SWAMI VIVEKANANDA: *Inspired Talks, 26 June 1895*

THOSE WHO give themselves up to the Lord do more for the world than the so-called workers. One man who has purified himself thoroughly accomplishes more than a regiment of preachers. Out of purity and silence comes the word of power. Be like a lily, stay in one place and expand your petals and the bees will come of themselves.

SWAMI VIVEKANANDA: *Inspired Talks, 26 June 1895*

IT IS bondage, when the mind desires anything or grieves about anything, rejects or welcomes anything, feels angry or happy about anything. Liberation is attained when the mind does not desire or grieve or reject or accept or feel happy or angry. It is bondage when the mind is attached to any particular sense organ. It is liberation when the mind is not attached to any sense organ. When there is no "I" there is liberation; where there is "I" there is bondage. Considering this, refrain from accepting or rejecting anything.

Ashtakavra Samhita, VIII

IS THE world real? Is it an illusion? With form? Without form? Conscious or unconscious? Is it joy or pain? Why worry about it! Search for your self! When you wake up, the world wakes up for you; when you fall asleep, where is it? First find out who it is through whom the world exists for you. Who is the knower? Who is ignorant? The one who knows? The one who knows not? What does it mean to know the self? Not to know the self? Knowledge and ignorance are only known in relation to each other. Knowledge of whom? Ignorance of what? This is the real question. No one is bound except by the ideas of "bound" and "unbound". Find out who is bound; if no one is bound, what then is liberation? Is liberation formless or with form? Or both with and without form? Thus discuss the pandits. When the I, that discusses it, is no more to be found, what has happened to "liberation"?

RAMANA MAHARSHI: *Ulladu Narpadu*

WE HAVE drunk Soma, we have become immortal; we have gone to the light, we have found the gods. What can hostility now do to us, and what the malice of mortal men, immortal one?

Rigveda, VII, 48, 3

THOSE WHO have gone to the beyond do not come back,
Nor do they send messages.
A saint, an ordinary person, a monk, a master,
A guru, a goddess, a god,
Ganesha, Brahma, Vishnu and Shiva,
All are whirling around in ever new births.
A yogi, a mendicant, an ascetic, a heaven-clad, a dervish,
A shaved one, one with matted hair, a pandit,
Inhabitants of the world below, the world above,
And all other worlds.
Philosophers, artists, poets,
People skilled in all kinds of things,
Kings and beggars – all go round.
Some praise Ram, others Rahim, others call out to Adesh.
Variegated as their costumes may be,
They are all whirled around in the four directions.
Kabir says: without the word of the *sadguru*
You will not reach your end.

KABIR: *Bahuri nakin*

THERE MAY be one or two people to whom I can
    explain it.
All have lost themselves in the business of the belly.
The horse is water, the rider is wind,
Like the dew-drop he will fall soon.
In a deep stream, carried away by an unfathomable
    current,
The boatman's pole is useless.
The "Thing" in the house does not strike the eye.
But the blind, who have lighted a lamp, are making a
    search.
The fire has caught on, the whole forest of the world
    is aflame.
Without a guru one goes astray.
Kabir says: listen brother monk!
You were born even without the loincloth around
    your body!

KABIR: *Kehi Samujharaun*

THE INNER VOICE

THERE COME to us moments in life when about some things we need no proof from without. A little voice within tells us, "You are on the right track, move neither to your left nor right, but keep to the straight and narrow way."

MAHATMA GANDHI: *The Leader, 25 Dec. 1916*

THERE ARE moments in your life when you must act even though you cannot carry your best friends with you. The "still small voice" within you must always be the final arbiter when there is a conflict of duty.

MAHATMA GANDHI: *Young India, 4 Aug. 1920*

I HAVE no special revelation of God's will. My firm belief is, that He reveals Himself daily to every human being, but we shut our ears to the still small voice. We shut our eyes to the Pillar of Fire in front of us. I realize His omnipresence.

MAHATMA GANDHI: *Young India, 25 May 1921*

SPIRITUALITY

THE NEED FOR A NEW SPIRITUALITY

A SPIRITUAL awareness and social efficiency are not only consistent but also complementary. To ignore the spiritual is to restrict one's capacity for effective social work. God is with the fence-breakers, the fermenters, the revolutionaries.

S. RADHAKRISHNAN: *East and West in Religion*, p. 105

THE NEW world order must have a deep spiritual impulse to give it unity and drive. It alone can give a rational basis to the social programme...There is no other source from which salvation can come to a world wandering ever more deeply into tragedy ... If we are centred in the spiritual reality we shall be freed from the greed and the fear which are the basis of our society which is anarchic and competitive. To change it into a human community in which everyone's physical and psychical advance is provided for, we have to enlarge our consciousness, recognize life's purpose and accept it in our own work.

S. RADHAKRISHNAN: *Religion and Society pp. 42 and 48*

THE REAL character of a civilization is to be gathered not so much from its forms and institutions as from the values of spirit, the furniture of the mind. Religion is the middle of a civilization, the soul as it were of the body of its social organization. Scientific applications, economic alliances, political institutions may bring the world together outwardly, but for a strong and stable unity the invisible but deeper bonds of ideas and ideals require to be strengthened. In the work of rebuilding the human household the role of religion is no less important than that of science. The human individual consists of body, mind and spirit. Each requires its proper nutriment. The body is kept trim by food and exercise, the mind is informed by science and criticism, and the spirit is illumined by art and literature, philosophy and religion.

S. RADHAKRISHNAN: *East and West in Religion*, pp. 44f.

INNER PEACE

ABANDONING ALL desires and acting free from longing, without any sense of mineness or sense of ego one attains to peace.

Bhagavadgita, II, 71

FAITH

IT IS faith that steers us through stormy seas, faith that moves mountains and faith that jumps across the ocean. That faith is nothing but a living, wide-awake consciousness of God within. He who has achieved that faith wants nothing. Bodily diseased, he is spiritually healthy; physically poor, he rolls in spiritual riches.

MAHATMA GANDHI: *Young India, 24 Sept. 1925*

A MAN wanted to cross a river. A sage gave him an amulet and said, "This will carry you across." The man, taking it in his hand, began to walk over the water. Before he had gone half the way, he was seized with curiosity, and opened the amulet to see what was in it. Therein he found, written on a piece of paper, the sacred name of Rama, the Lord. At this the man said depreciatingly, "Is this the whole secret?" No sooner did this scepticism enter his mind than he sank down. It is faith in the Name of the Lord that works wonders; for faith is life and want of faith is death.

Sayings of Shri Ramakrishna, No. 506

TRUTH

TRUTH AND Love is the only thing that counts. Where this is present, everything rights itself in the end. This is a law to which there is no exception.

MAHATMA GANDHI: *Young India, 18 Aug. 1927*

TRUTH IS like a vast tree which yields more and more fruit, the more you nurture it. The deeper the search is in the mine of truth, the richer the discovery of the gems buried there, in the shape of openings for an ever greater variety of service.

MAHATMA GANDHI: *Autobiography, p. 159*

I THINK it is wrong to expect certainties in this world, where all else but God that is Truth is an uncertainty. All that appears and happens about and around is uncertain, transient. But there is a Supreme Being hidden therein as a Certainty, and one would be blessed if one could catch a glimpse of that certainty and hitch one's waggon to it. The quest for that Truth is the highest good in life.

MAHATMA GANDHI: *Autobiography, p. 184*

ONE SHOULD speak Truth that is consistent with righteousness. There is nothing higher than that Truth. Where untruth would assume the character of Truth, Truth should not be said. There, again where Truth would assume the character of untruth, even untruth should be said. That ignorant person incurs sin who utters Truth dissociated from righteousness. When life is at risk, or at the occasion of marriage, one may say an untruth. One that seeks virtue does not commit a sin by saying an untruth, if that untruth is said to save the prosperity and wealth of others or for religious purposes.

Mahabharata, XII, 110

TRUTH CREATES all creatures and by Truth the whole universe is upheld, with the help of Truth one goes to heaven. Untruth is Darkness, it leads to hell. Those afflicted by Darkness and covered by it fail to behold the lighted regions of heaven. Heaven is Light and hell is Darkness.

Mahabharata, XII, 190

NOBODY CAN throw back with force the approaching army of the god of death; Truth alone can do that, since immortality is grounded in Truth.

Mahabharata, XII, 169

THROUGH TRUTH the sun is shining and through Truth the moon is waxing, out of Truth came the draught of immortality and on Truth the world is founded. The regions which those who live in Truth enter by means of Truth will never be reached by those who live in untruth, even if they offered hundreds of sacrifices.

Ramayana, II, 61

TRUTH IS by nature self-evident. As soon as you remove the cobwebs of ignorance that surround it, it shines clear.

MAHATMA GANDHI: Young India, 27 May 1926

IF YOU would swim on the bosom of the ocean of Truth you must reduce yourself to a zero.

MAHATMA GANDHI: Young India, 31 Dec. 1931

W HAT THEN is Truth? A difficult question, but I have solved it for myself by saying that it is what the voice within tells you.

MAHATMA GANDHI: *Young India, 31 Dec. 1931*

FEARLESSNESS

FEARLESSNESS IS the first requisite of spirituality. Cowards can never be moral.

MAHATMA GANDHI: *Young India, 13 Oct. 1921*

VICES

A SAINT comes to grief through greed, a king through bad counsel, a woman through drink, nobility through wicked offspring, a brahmin through neglect of study, a farm through neglect, a friendship through lack of respect, a love through absence, a fortune through careless spending.

Pancatantra, I

SOMEONE STEPPING off the path of righteousness in pursuit of wickedness will not only suffer misfortune but also much remorse. Someone not heeding a sincere friend's sound advice will not only make his enemies smile but also pay the price for his folly.

Pancatantra, II

ANGER

INNUMERABLE PEOPLE are angry without any reason; a large number are angry for a reason; there are only a few who are not getting angry even if they have a reason.

Subhashitarnava, 83

GREED

A s THE horn grows with growing cattle, so greed grows with growing riches.

Mahabharata, XI, 268

AMBITION

As THE honey-thirsty bee who alights on the lotus while the sun is setting is unaware that the flower will become a trap when night is falling, so a recognition-hungry ambitious person is oblivious of all dangers.

Pancatantra, II

FOLLY

IN FIGHTING there is no wisdom; it is only fools that fight. The wise find in their scriptures the right course: non-violence.

Pancatantra, II

TO ENTER a house uninvited, to talk without being asked, to praise oneself and to run down others – these four are the signs of a featherbrain.

Subhashitarnava, 193

PRIDE

BEAUTY IS ruined by old age, deliberation by desire, life by death, the fulfilment of duties by grumbling, shame by love, good manners by service to unworthy people, grace by anger; everything, however, is ruined by pride.

Mahabharata, V, 35

VIRTUES

THE GOOD is one thing, and another thing is the pleasant. Serving different ends these two bind the soul. One who follows the good does well, but one who chooses the pleasant misses the aim. Both the good and the pleasant are laid out before us. The wise discern between these two after having examined them. The wise prefer the good to the pleasant, but those of little understanding choose the pleasant out of avarice and attachment.

Katha Upanishad, II, 1–2

FORTITUDE, FORGIVENESS, self-control, abstention from unlawful gain, purity of body and mind, sense-control, study of scriptures, meditation on the Supreme, truthfulness, freedom from anger – this is the tenfold path of virtue.

Manusmriti, VI, 92

WISDOM

A SAGE'S mind is not troubled in the midst of sorrows, without desire amidst pleasures, free from passion, fear and rage, without affection, not rejoicing at the sight of good nor revolting at the sight of evil.

Bhagavadgita, II, 56–7

WISDOM IS regarded as the highest of acquisitions. Wisdom is the highest felicity in the world. Wisdom is heaven in the opinion of the good and virtuous.

Mahabharata, XIII, 180

THOSE WHO have understood the connection between all things do not shed tears; for the one who looks at everything with right understanding there are no tears.

Mahabharata, XII, 317

A TREE that has been cut off grows again; the waning moon is waxing again. Wise people who contemplate this are not vexed by misfortunes.

Bhartrihari, II, 84

W ISDOM IS the boat that carries us across the dark sea of wrong doctrines; wisdom is the eye of the world; wisdom is a tall mountain on the banks of the river of right behaviour; wisdom is the remover of flaws of character; wisdom is the secret *mantra* in the endeavour for emancipation; wisdom is the purifier of the heart; wisdom is the drum that is sounded at the time of departure for heaven; wisdom is the cause of the highest felicity.

Subhashitarnava, 281

T HE SAGE who enjoys wisdom and who entertains no enmity towards any creature does not know fear of rebirth nor fear of the world beyond.

Mahabharata, XII, 54

PATIENCE

CONTACT WITH sense objects gives rise to the feeling of cold and hot, pleasure and pain. These come and go and do not last forever. Learn to endure these. One who is not troubled by these, who remains the same in cold and heat, pleasure and pain, is wise.

Bhagavadgita, II, 14–15

IF THERE were no patient people resembling the earth, there would be no peace, since anger is the root cause of all discord. The one who had been cursed, would curse back, and the one who had been struck would strike back: in this way creatures would perish and the law with them.

Mahabharata, III, 20

DO NOT be despondent because of ill-fate; there cannot be sesame-oil without crushing the sesame seeds.

Pancatantra, II

D O NOT seek revenge against those who have done you evil; they will fall by themselves like trees on the banks of a river.

Pancatantra, I

A WATERPOT is filled by the steady fall of single drops; it is similar with the growth of knowledge, character and wealth.

Vriddha Canakya, 12, 22

HUMILITY

THINK OF yourself as less significant than a blade of grass, be more forbearing than a tree, do not desire to be honoured but render honour to others, always sing the praise of Hari's name.

O Lord of the universe, I do not desire wealth, children, a beautiful wife or a poet's gift: may I have, in life after life, disinterested love towards you!

O you, son of Nanda! I really am your servant but I have been thrown into the ocean of *samsara*, full of opposites. Have mercy on me and consider me a particle of dust clinging to your lotus feet.

CAITANYA: *Shikshashtaka, 3 and 4*

DISCIPLINE

WHEN ONE dwells in one's mind on sense objects, attachment to them arises. From attachment springs desire, from desire rises anger. From anger follows bewilderment, from bewilderment comes loss of memory, loss of memory causes the destruction of intelligence; from destruction of intelligence one perishes. A disciplined mind, moving among the sense objects, with senses under control and free from attachment and aversion, attains purity of spirit. That purity of spirit brings to an end all sorrow.

Bhagavadgita, II, 62–5

ON DISCIPLINE depend all creatures. The learned therefore say that discipline is the root of everything. Upon discipline rests the heaven that men desire, and upon it rests his world too. Where discipline is well applied there is no wickedness, no sin, no deception. If the rod of discipline is not uplifted, the dog will lick the sacrificial butter and the crow will carry away the offerings.

Mahabharata, XII, 15

IF A RULER did not readily punish those that deserve punishment the stronger would fry like fish on a stick the weaker ones, the crow would eat the sacrifical rice and the dog would lick the butter offering; nothing would anymore be one's own and everything would become topsy-turvy.

Manusmriti, VII, 20

GOOD DEEDS

CHARITY, DOING good! How dare you say you can do good to others? Kindness belongs to God alone. How can a man lay claim to it? Charity depends on the Will of Rama. If a householder gives in charity in a spirit of detachment, he is really doing good to himself and not to others. It is God alone that he serves – God who dwells in all beings, and when he serves God through all beings he is really doing good to himself and not to others.

The Gospel of Ramakrishna, p. 641

LIFE MOVES on like a wind, power is like a rainbow of short duration, youth is like a flash without permanence, wealth is rushing down like the waves of a torrent, bodily vigour collapses like an elephant's ears, the body is visited by diseases: understanding all that, do good works that are pure and lasting.

Subhashitarnava, 88

THERE IS a trifle fear or greed or selfishness in every good deed.

Pancatantra, II

FOUR GIFTS the wise have declared to bring salvation in this world and the next: the gift of safety for the frightened, the gift of medicine for the sick, the gift of knowledge for those who want to learn, and the gift of food for the hungry.

Subhashitarnava, 30

THAT IS the whole purpose of human existence here on earth: to benefit other people through one's life, one's possessions, one's thoughts and one's words.

Bhagavata Purana, X, 22, 35

THOSE WHO care for animals and plants like for themselves will obtain the highest heaven.

Subhashitarnava, 16

AMBHU MALLICK once talked about establishing hospitals, dispensaries and schools, making roads, digging public reservoirs, and so forth. I said to him: "Don't go out of your way to look for such works. Undertake only those works that present themselves to you and are of pressing necessity – and those also in a spirit of detachment." It is not good to become involved in many activities. That makes one forget God. Work is only a means to the realization of God. Therefore I said to Sambhu: "Suppose, God appears before you, then will you ask Him to build hospitals and dispensaries for you? A lover of God never says that. He will rather say: 'O Lord, give me a place at your Lotus Feet. Keep me always in your company. Give me sincere and pure love for you.' "

The Gospel of Ramakrishna, pp. 641f.

SOMEONE WHO fails to earn by means of this transient body either fame or merit through kindness to living beings deserves to be pitied even by plants and trees. The great virtue practised by sages of renown consisted in their grieving and rejoicing in sympathy with the grief and joy of their fellow-beings. What a pity that people should not serve others with their wealth, children, relations and their bodies, which are not only transient and of no use to them but really belong to others.

Bhagavata Purana, VI, 10

TAKE HANUMAN as your example in *seva* [service]. He served Rama, the Prince of Righteousness, regardless of obstacles of all types. Though he was strong, learned and virtuous, he had no trace of pride. When asked who he was by the Rakshakas in Lanka into which he had entered so daringly, he described himself, in all humility, as "the servant of Rama". That is a fine example of uprooting of the ego, which *seva* must bring about in us. No one can serve another while his ego is rampant. The attitudes of mutual help and selfless service develop the "humanness" of man and help the unfoldment of the divinity latent in him.

Sathya Sai Speaks, XI, 192

THE BULLOCK of the oil machine goes round and round its limited circle for the whole day, and in spite of his hard labour, he remains where he was, and does not advance even an inch. Similarly the worldly man remains engrossed in his family affairs, day and night, like the bullock of an oil machine, but does not know where he is going to and what he is aiming at. Yes, but at the time of his death, when he realizes that he has wasted his whole life for nothing, it is then too late. He then weeps and repents for his failure, but in vain. Ultimately he dies in pain and anguish with repentance. O man, engrossed in family snares, remember that this world is not the place of rest. Here you have to work and to be progressive. Spread your hands to embrace others. Increase your fellow-feeling and love for all, so that your limited circle of selfish life may expand unlimitedly to become a straight line, and so that your life may follow the straight path of righteousness. Advance, advance and be progressive, till you leave this transitory world and its affairs far behind.

SWAMI RAMA TIRTHA: *In Woods of God-Realization*, V, *141*

PRUDENCE

DO NOT entertain thoughts of revenge unless you are capable of action – the chick-pea, hopping up and down, will not break the pan it is fried in.

Pancatantra, I

ONE SHOULD approach with great care these six: fire, water, women, fools, snakes and rulers – they can easily take one's life.

Vriddha Canakya, 14, 12

ONE SHOULD engage in the acquisition of learning and wealth as if one did not age and decay; one should practise virtue as if death had already caught one at one's hair.

Canakya, 11

IF WE had to choose between a son who had not been born, a son who had died and a foolish son, we should choose the first two and not the latter: these cause pain but once, that one at every step.

Pancatantra, IV

OFTEN THE true seems false and the false true. Appearances deceive – think about it.

Pancatantra, II

DISCRETION

EVERY UNSUITABLE gift is lost and so is every service rendered to dull people. Kindness is not repaid by the ungrateful and courtesy is not appreciated by the uncultured.

Pancatantra, II

THESE NINE things one should keep secret: one's age, one's wealth, an opening in the wall, one's love, one's medicine, one's religious exercises, one's charity, and the insults one has suffered.

Hitopadesha, I

PIETY

THE WORSHIP of mother, father and preceptor is most important. The man who attends to that duty succeeds in acquiring great fame in this world and regions of bliss in the next. Whatever they command, be it consistent with righteousness or not, should always be done. One should never do what they forbid. What they command should always be done. They are the three worlds. They are the three modes of life. They are the three Vedas. They are the three sacred fires.

Mahabharata, XII, 109

ONE WHO honours his father honours the creator himself. One who honours his mother, honours the earth herself. One who honours the teacher, honours the Supreme Being by this very act. For this reason the teacher is worthy of greater reverence than father or mother. Father and mother only create the body. The life which one obtains from the teacher, however, is heavenly. That life is not subject to decay and mortality.

Mahabharata, XII, 109

INTELLIGENCE

I T IS a sign of the intelligent to understand quickly, to listen carefully, not to be prompted to action as soon as something had been understood, and not to mind someone else's business without having been asked.

Mahabharata, V, 33

CONTENTMENT

CONTENTMENT IS the highest heaven, contentment is the highest bliss. There is nothing higher than contentment. When one withdraws all desires like a tortoise withdraws its limbs, then the natural splendour of the soul soon manifests itself. When one does not fear any creature, nor any creature is frightened by one, when one conquers both one's desires and aversions, then one is said to behold one's soul. When one seeks not to injure anybody in word or deed and cherishes no desire, one is said to attain the Highest.

Mahabharata, XII, 21

THE CONTENT lives happily with whatever fate may bring; the discontent, not having self-mastery, is not happy even when winning the three worlds.

Bhagavata Purana, VIII, 19

HOSPITALITY

EVEN AN enemy must be offered appropriate hospitality, if he comes to your home. A tree does not deny its shade to the one who comes to cut it down.

Mahabharata, XII, 374

THE WORLD

THEN THERE was neither being nor non-being, neither air nor sky. What was moving about, where, and under whose protection? What was the impenetrably deep water?

Then there was neither death nor immortality, there was no sign of day or night. According to its own nature the One was breathing without a wind. Besides this there was no other.

In the beginning there was darkness enveloped by darkness; all this was an indistinguishable dark mass of water. The lifeforce was enclosed by the void, the one was born through the power of its inner urge.

In the beginning desire entered it, the first seed of thought. Searching in their hearts, by deep pondering the sages found that being was tied to non-being.

They stretched their measuring thread across. Was there an above, a below? There were creative powers and forces of expansion; beneath was desire, above fulfilment.

Who knows for certain, and who can tell for sure whence it originated and where this world came from? The gods were born after this world's creation: who can know from whence it has arisen?

Whence this world has come, and whether He, the Overseer made it or not – he alone knows and does not know.

Rigveda, X, 129

THE WORLD is real for the ignorant as well as for the wise; for the ignorant the Real is measured by the world, for one who knows the Real has no limits and is the foundation of the world. Both say "I" referring to themselves – the ignorant and the one who knows. For the ignorant the self is defined by the body, the wise knows that within the body the unlimited Self shines with its own splendour.

RAMANA MAHARSHI: *Ulladu Narpadu*

ALL IS VANITY

WHEN THE leaves have separated from the tree
They cannot be fastened back on it again by any
   device.
In the state of delirium
Phlegm will obstruct your throat, your tongue will fail,
Yama will come to snatch away your life-breath.
Mother and father look on in bewilderment
One moment will appear to you like a thousand
   aeons.
Your love of the world is like the love of a parrot
For the fruit of the silk-cotton tree.
When it touches it with its beak the cotton will fly
   away.
O madman, do not fall into Yama's trap!
Let your mind rest at the feet of God.
Sur says that this body is useless
Why do you carry so much conceit in your heart?

SURDAS: *Re man, I, 14*

STUCK LIKE a fly in the thing-juice, yet far from understanding
He has lost the diamond "God" in the midst of his house.
He is like a deer that sees mirages that do not quench thirst,
Even if approached from ten different directions.
Having produced much karma in life after life in which he fettered himself.
He is like the parrot, who pinned his hope
On the fruit of the silk-cotton tree
Day and night he thought of it.
When he took it into his beak
The shell was empty and the cotton flew up and away.
He is like a monkey, tied on a rope by a juggler
Who makes him dance for a few grains at every corner.
Surdas says: without devotion to God
You will become just a morsel to eat for the tiger Time.

SURDAS: *Dhokhai hi dhokai*

MONEY

MONEY CAUSES pain when earned, it causes pain to keep and it causes pain to lose as well as to spend.

Pancatantra, I

IF YOU have wealth you have friends; if you have wealth you have relations; if you have wealth you are somebody; if you have wealth you are even considered learned.

Mahabharata, XII, 8

OTHER PEOPLE

PEOPLE WORSHIP those who have wrought great havoc; snakes receive worship, not Garuda, who exterminates them.

Pancatantra, I

ONE SHOULD defeat an angry man with meekness, an evil one with goodness, a miser with generosity, a liar with truth.

Mahabharata, V, 39

A NOBLE person treats another's fault as Shiva did with the poison: he does not spit it out from his mouth but lets it glide down to the heart and dissolves it.

Subhashitarnava, 275

ONE SHOULD repay a good deed with a good deed and an insult with an insult. I see nothing wrong in doing harm to an evildoer.

Pancatantra, V

ONE SHOULD act towards another person as that person has acted: someone devious should be treated with deviousness, someone sincere with sincerity.

Mahabharata, V, 37

ON THE tip of the tongue is seated the Goddess of Fortune, on the tip of the tongue resides the Goddess of Speech. On the tip of the tongue are located imprisonment and death, on the tip of the tongue is found the ultimate fate.

Subhashitarnava, 193

NO ENEMY, no weapon, no poison, no terrible illness can upset someone like harsh words. No moon, no water, no sandalwood paste, no cool shade refresh someone like sweet words.

Subhashitarnava, 286

ONE SHOULD get rid of one enemy by means of another enemy, whom one has done a good turn, as one removes a thorn from one's foot with the aid of another thorn.

Canakya, 22

SIX KINDS of people think little of those who formerly served them: students of their teachers, married sons of their mothers, disaffected men of their wives, the successful of their supporters, those who have left the woods of signposts, the sick who have recovered of their physicians.

Mahabharata, V, 183

HUMAN VALUES

As our enslavement to the economic machine is rising, human values are declining. We are at war with others, because we are at war with ourselves. The uprooted individual, mindless, traditionless, believes in anything or nothing. Scepticism and superstition hold the field. As he has no inward being, his surface nature is moulded by widespread and insistent propaganda. Any self-constituted saviour of society, who promises to provide food and shelter at the price of subjection to his leadership, wins a following. The establishments of dictatorships and the increasing supremacy of the State even in democracies are characteristic features of our time. With its ever growing reliance on objective criteria of thought and ever deepening ignorance of the real nature of human life, contemporary technological civilization has become a social disease. We see on all sides the apotheosis of power and the withering of man who has been cut off from the sources of self renewal.

S. RADHAKRISHNAN: *Fragments of a Confession, p. 22*

RELIGION

MEN MAY partition their lands by measuring rods and boundary lines, but no one can so partition the all-embracing sky overhead. The sky surrounds all and includes all. So the unenlightened man in his ignorance says that his religion is the only true one and that it is the best. But when his heart is illumined by the light of true knowledge, he comes to know that above all these wars of sects and creeds is the one Existence-Knowledge-Bliss.

Sayings of Shri Ramakrishna No. 474

HINDUISM IS not limited in scope to the geographical area which is described as India. There is nothing which prevents it from extending to the uttermost parts of the earth. India is a tradition, a spirit, a light. Her physical and spiritual frontiers do not coincide.

S. RADHAKRISHNAN: *Religion and Society p. 102*

LET ME explain what I mean by religion. It is not the Hindu religion, which I certainly prize above all other religions, but the religion which transcends Hinduism, which changes one's very nature, which binds one indissolubly to the truth within and which ever purifies. It is the permanent element in human nature which counts no cost too great in order to find full expression and which leaves the soul utterly restless until it has found itself, known its Maker and appreciated the true correspondence between the Maker and itself.

MAHATMA GANDHI: *quoted by J.J. Doke, M.K. Gandhi: An Indian Patriot in South Africa, p. 7*

THERE ARE several bathing *ghats* in a large tank. Whoever goes choosing whichever *ghat* he pleases to take a bath or to fill his vessel reaches the water and it is useless to quarrel with one another by calling one's *ghat* better than another. Similarly there are many *ghats* that lead to the water of the fountain of Eternal Bliss. Every religion of the world is one such *ghat*. Go direct with a sincere and earnest heart through any of these *ghats* and you shall reach the water of Eternal Bliss. But say not that your religion is better than that of another.

Sayings of Shri Ramakrishna, No. 462

IF WE are imperfect ourselves, religion, as conceived by us, must also be imperfect. We have not realized religion in its perfection even as we have not realized God. All faiths constitute a revelation of Truth but all are imperfect and liable to error. Reverence for other faiths need not blind us to their faults. Looking at all religions with an equal eye, we would not only not hesitate but would think it our duty to blend into our faith every acceptable feature of other faiths. Even as a tree has a single trunk, but many branches and leaves, so there is one true and perfect religion, but it becomes many, as it passes through the human medium. The one Religion is beyond all speech.

MAHATMA GANDHI: *From Yeravda Mandir, p. 55*

TO MAKE all life religion and to govern all activities by the religious idea would seem to be the right way to the development of the ideal individual and ideal society and the lifting of the whole life of man into the Divine.

SHRI AUROBINDO: *The Human Cycle p. 192*

A SPIRITUAL RELIGION of humanity is the hope of the future. By this is not meant what is ordinarily called a universal religion, a system, a thing of creed and intellectual belief and dogma and outward rite. Mankind has tried unity by that means; it has failed and deserved to fail, because there can be no universal religious system, one in the mental creed and in the vital form. The inner spirit is indeed one, but more than any other the spiritual life insists on freedom and variation in its self-expression and means of development. A religion of humanity means the growing realisation that there is a secret spirit, a Divine Reality, in which we are all one, that humanity is its highest present vehicle on earth, that the human race and the human being are the means by which it will progressively reveal itself here. It implies a growing attempt to live out this knowledge and bring about a kingdom of this Divine Spirit upon earth.

By its growth within us oneness with our fellow-men will become the leading principle of co-operation, but a deeper brotherhood, a real and an inner sense of unity and equality and a common life. There must be the realisation by the individual that only in the life of his fellow-men is his own life complete. There must be the realisation by the race that only on the free and full life of the individual can its own perfection and permanent happiness be founded. There must be too a discipline and a way of salvation in accordance with this religion, that is to say, a means by which it can be developed by each man within himself so that it may be developed in the life of the race.

SHRI AUROBINDO: *The Ideal of Human Unity, pp. 322ff.*

HINDUISM REPRESENTS an effort of comprehension and co-operation. It recognizes the diversities in man's approach towards, and realisation of, the one Supreme Reality. For it the essence of religion consists in man's hold on what is eternal and immanent in all being. Its validity does not depend on historical happenings.

S. RADHAKRISHNAN: *Religion and Society, p. 52*

THE MYSTIC religion of India, which affirms that things spiritual are personal and that we have to reflect them in our lives, which requires us to withdraw from the world's concerns to find the real and return with renewed energy and certitude to the world, which is at once spiritual and social, is likely to be the religion of the new world, which will draw men to a common centre even across the national frontiers.

S. RADHAKRISHNAN: *Religion and Society, p. 49*

IN THE present crisis, the spiritual forces of the world must come together and the great religious traditions should transcend their differences of form, underline their basic unity and draw from it the strength necessary to counter materialistic determinism.

S. RADHAKRISHNAN: *East and West in Religion, p. 207*

CIVILIZATION IS in its infancy and religion yet in the making. Human progress is to be defined as the process by which society is transformed increasingly in a spiritual way. The world is unfinished and it is the task of religion to go forward with the task of refining it. On this view religion is not quiescent but combative, exposing the hostility and hollowness of the irreligious principle. It means a profound dissatisfaction with the existing state of humanity and an active preparation for a new life... Religion is an eternal revolutionary because no order of life can ever satisfy it. It demands that most radical transformation of man and society. It will not be content until a new social order with basic economic justice, racial brotherhood and equality, true intellectual and spiritual co-operation and true friendship among nations is established...It is not enough to change outward forms and institutions. We must transform the feelings and passions of men.

S. RADHAKRISHNAN: *Contemporary Indian Philosophy, p. 504*

EDUCATION

ONE SHOULD treat one's son for five years like a prince, for ten years like a slave, on reaching the sixteenth year, like a friend.

Popular Proverb

INTELLECTUAL KNOWLEDGE is partial, because our intellect is an instrument, it is only part of us, it can give us information about things which can be divided and analysed, and whose properties can be classified, part by part. But Brahma is perfect, and knowledge which is partial can never be a knowledge of him. But he can be known by joy, by love. For joy is knowledge in its completeness, it is knowing by our whole being. Intellect sets us apart from the things to be known, but love knows its object by fusion. Such knowledge is immediate and admits no doubt. It is the same as knowing our own selves, only more so.

RABINDRANATH TAGORE: *Sadhana, p. 159*

A PURELY scientific education tends to make keen and clear-sighted within certain limits, but narrow, hard and cold. Man, intellectually developed, mighty in scientific knowledge and the mastery of the gross and subtle nature, using the elements as his servants and the world as his footstool, but underdeveloped in heart and spirit, becomes only an inferior kind of *asura* [demon] using the powers of a demigod to satisfy the nature of an animal.

SHRI AUROBINDO: *The Dharma, 27 Nov. 1909*

THE GREAT crimes against civilization are committed not by the primitive and uneducated but by the highly educated and so-called civilized. Any satisfactory system of education should aim at the balanced growth of the individual and insist on both knowledge and wisdom. It should not only train the intellect but bring grace to the heart of man. If we do not have a general philosophy or attitude of life our minds will be confused and we will suffer from greed, pusillanimity, anxiety and defeatism. Mental slums are more dangerous than material slums.

S. RADHAKRISHNAN: *Occasional Speeches and Writings, I, 60*

ONE WHO desires true (spiritual) wealth and prosperity must secure the help of a teacher with these qualifications: he must be firmly attached to and take his stand on the worthy and proper tradition; he must be possessed of steady and unflinching intellect; he must be free from blemish; he must have mastered the Vedas; he must be deeply attached to the Lord and live, move and have his being in him; he must be firmly established in goodness; he must always speak the truth and truth only; he must possess good conduct; he must be free from vanity, jealousy and other vices; he must keep his senses under control; he must be a lifelong close relation; he must be full of mercy and compassion; he must never hesitate to point out lapses of conduct; he must always act in a manner conducive to his own and others' welfare.

The teacher should be venerated and worshipped as if he were the Lord himself. For both possess the same qualities: they dispel the darkness of ignorance; they wipe out sins; they bring into existence their own qualities; they confer new life which does away with the old one; they possess the efficacy and power of divine vision; they have unbounded compassion; they are ever sweet and are forever in command. The disciple must be convinced that the teachings of the spiritual guide are beyond remuneration.

VEDANTA DESHIKA: *Nyasa Vimshati, 1–3*

A GOOD student must have a good intellect, be respectful towards holy people, be of good conduct, desirous to learn about the true nature of things and men, render faithful service to the master, must not feel self-important, respect the master, await the proper time and opportunity to place his questions and doubts before the master, keep his senses under control, control his mind, be not jealous, have faith in the traditional teaching, be tested by the master and be grateful.

VEDANTA DESHIKA: *Nyasa Vimshati, 4*

E DUCATION IS man's perennial birth in the spirit, it is the road to the inward kingdom.

S. RADHAKRISHNAN: *Religion and Society, p. 41*

OUR CIVILIZATION

WE CANNOT base the new civilization on science and technology alone. They do not furnish a reliable foundation. We must learn to live from a new basis, if we wish to avoid the catastrophe which threatens us. We must discover the reserves of spirituality, the sense of the sacred found in all religious traditions and use them to fashion a new type of man who uses the instruments he has invented with a renewed awareness that he is capable of greater things than mastery of nature. The service to which man must return is man himself, the spirit in him.

S. RADHAKRISHNAN: *East and West in Religion*, *p. 209*

THE CRISIS which faces us today is not an intellectual crisis but a spiritual one. Unless egoism in all its forms, tribal, racial, national, bends to the dominion of love and goodness, our future is not safe.

Unfortunately in our educational institutions we feed the animal, train the mind but do not attend to the spirit in man. We listen to the radio, see the cinema or television, read the newspaper, repeat slogans, absorb the impressions we are given. We become a set of mirrors reflecting whatever is presented to us. We are empty within and drift on a tide of trivialities, automatic actions, conditioned responses that do not reach any significant level of intensity. We do not find any purpose or meaning in life. We become like one of these machines we handle, and are satisfied with sex, drink or the national flag. As our inward resources are depleted, we depend on external diversions. We are fragmented beings, afraid of ourselves.

S.RADHAKRISHNAN: *Address to Gandhi Memorial Academy,*
Nairobi, 12 July 1956

EVERYWHERE AROUND us we hear the sounds of things breaking, of changes in the social, in the political and economic situations, in the dominant beliefs and ideas, in the fundamental categories of human mind. Men of intelligence, sensitiveness and enterprise are convinced that there is something radically wrong with the present arrangements and institutions in regard to politics, economics and industry, and that we must get rid of them if we are to save humanity.

S. RADHAKRISHNAN: *Religion and Society, p. 10*

THE CRISIS of the time lies in our acquisition of vast new powers over the world of nature without acquiring any more power over ourselves. The problem facing us is: why has man not grown in moral character as well as in intellectual power? Why is he obsessed by unrelenting hatred and unceasing fears? Flight from spiritual life accounts partly for the frenzy of our time. We suffer today not so much from the split atom as from the split mind.

S. RADHAKRISHNAN: *Address to Saugar University, 11 Feb. 1954*

SOCIETY

WHERE THE mind is without fear – and the head is held high, where knowledge is free; where the world has not been broken up into fragments by narrow domestic walls, where words come out from the depth of Truth, where tireless striving stretches its arms towards perfection, where the clear stream of reason has not lost its way into the dreary desert sand of dead habit, where the mind is led forward by thee into ever-widening thought and action – into that heaven of freedom my Father, let my country wake.

RABINDRANATH TAGORE: *Gitanjali, No. 36*

FREEDOM AND harmony express the two necessary principles of variation and oneness – freedom of the individual, the group, the race, co-ordinated harmony of the individual's forces and of the efforts of all the individuals in the group, of all groups in the race, of all races in the kind – and these are the two conditions of healthy progression and successful arrival.

SHRI AUROBINDO: *The Human Cycle, p. 84*

THUS THE community stands as a mid-term and intermediary value between the individual and humanity and it exists not merely for itself, but for the one and the other and to help them to fulfil each other. The individual has to live in humanity as well as humanity in the individual, but mankind is or has been too large an aggregate to make this mutuality a thing intimate and powerfully felt in the ordinary mind of the race, and even if humanity becomes a manageable unit of life, intermediate groups and aggregates must still exist for the purpose of mass-differentiation and the concentration and combination of varying tendencies in the total human aggregate. Therefore the community has to stand for a time to the individual for humanity even at the cost of standing between him and it and limiting the reach of his universality and the wideness of his sympathies.

SHRI AUROBINDO: *The Human Cycle, pp. 88*

THE TRUE and full spiritual aim in society will regard man not as a mind, a life and a body, but as a soul incarnated for a divine fulfilment upon earth, not only in heavens beyond, which after all it need not have left if it had no divine business here in the world of physical, vital and mental nature. It will therefore regard the life, mind and body neither as ends in themselves, sufficient for their own satisfaction, nor as mortal members full of disease which only have to be dropped off for the rescued spirit to flee away into its own pure regions, but as first instruments of the soul, the yet imperfect instruments of an unseized diviner purpose.

SHRI AUROBINDO: *The Human Cycle, p. 305*

A LARGE liberty will be the law of a spiritual society and the increase of freedom a sign of the growth of human society towards the possibility of true spiritualization.

SHRI AUROBINDO: *The Human Cycle, p. 306*

THE STATE

THE STATE exists for the freedom and responsible life of the individuals. It consists of and exists for individual persons. Life is manifested in individuals. Truth is revealed to the individual. He learns and suffers, he knows joy and sorrow, forgiveness and hatred. He enjoys the thrill of his victories and suffers the anguish of his failures. It is his right to live his life to the full, with all its ecstasies and shudders. It is his privilege to be eccentric, wayward, unorthodox, non-conformist. The world owes its progress to men who are ill at ease...The inviolate sanctity of the human soul, the freedom of the human spirit, is the sole justification for the State. We are born separately and die separately and in our essential life we are alone. The State must protect the dharma of individuals and groups.

B. RADHAKRISHNAN: *Religion and Society*, p. 60

179

THE MEANING OF HISTORY

THE GOD who is responsible for this world, who is the consciousness of the universe, is working through brute matter from which he has to liberate himself, and liberate us. He himself is suffering in each and all of us. This suffering will be at an end, when the spirit which is imprisoned in transitory matter is released, when the potential world spirit of the whole becomes the actual consciousness of each part, when God becomes "all in all" – when the solitary limited God becomes the Pantheistic God.

S. RADHAKRISHNAN: *East and West in Religion, p. 124*

LIFE ETERNAL is to be realized on this earth itself. Love of man is as fundamental to religion as worship of God. We must seek our evolution through the medium of this life, by transforming it, by changing it over.

S. RADHAKRISHNAN: *East and West in Religion, p. 105*

HUMAN DESIRES are the means by which the ideal becomes actual. The world is not a mistake or an illusion to be cast aside but a scene of spiritual evolution by which, out of the material the divine consciousness may be manifested.

The cosmos is working out a great possibility of reaching spiritual oneness through the exercise of human freedom, with all its consequences of danger and difficulty, pain and imperfection.

S. RADHAKRISHNAN: *Religion and Society*, *pp. 103f.*

THE MEANING of history is to make all men prophets, to establish a kingdom of free spirits. The infinitely rich and spiritually impregnated future, this drama of the gradual transmutation of intellect into spirit, of the son of man into the son of God, is the goal of history. When death is overcome, when time is conquered, the kingdom of the eternal spirit is established.

S. RADHAKRISHNAN: *Fragments of a Confession, p. 30*

MAN'S HISTORY is the history of his journey to the unknown in quest of the realization of his immortal self – his soul.

RABINDRANATH TAGORE: *The Religion of Man*, p. 64

GOD, THOUGH immanent, is not identical with the world until the very end. Throughout the process there is an unrealized residuum in God, but it vanishes when we reach the end, when the reign is absolute the kingdom comes. God who is organic with it recedes into the background of the Absolute.

S. RADHAKRISHNAN: *An Idealist View of Life*, p. 340

MAY WE not prepare for the truth of the world's yet unborn soul by a free interchange of ideas and the development of a philosophy which will combine the best of European humanism and Asiatic Religion, a philosophy profounder and more living than either, endowed with greater spiritual and ethical force which will conquer the hearts of men and compel peoples to acknowledge its sway?

S. RADHAKRISHNAN: *Fragments of a Confession*, p. 7

MISCELLANEA

THE ROOT of wealth is cunning and patience; the root of love is beauty and youth; the root of virtue is compassion and self-control; the root of emancipation is the performance of good deeds.

Subhashitarnava, 105

A KING from a low family, a scholar who is a fool's son, and a poor man who has become rich look at the world as if it was a blade of dry grass.

Subhashitarnava, 219

IF UNIMPORTANT people are asked about something in some affair by an important person they consider themselves important, and the important person unimportant.

Mahabharata, V, 34

THESE SEVEN one should not wake up when asleep: a snake, a ruler, a tiger, an old man, a child, someone else's dog and a fool.

Vriddha Canakya, 9, 7

ONE COMES to know a friend in misfortune, a hero in a battle, an honest man in debts, a spouse at the loss of one's property and relations in discomfort.

Hitopadesha, I, 66

BY FLEEING from misfortune, from a hostile army, from a dreadful famine and from the society of wicked people one saves one's life.

Vriddha Canakya, 3, 19

STUPIDITY IS an aggravation, and so is poverty in youth. The worst aggravation, however, is living in someone else's house and in a foreign country.

Subhashitarnava, 120

IN WINTER the clouds make thunder but do not give rain; during the rainy season the clouds give rain without thunder. Common people talk without acting; highminded people act without talking.

Subhashitarnava, 2090

HERE WE have the sound of music, there the clamour of unfortunates; here we have a debate between scholars, there we have a quarrel between drunks; here we have an attractive beauty, there we have a body broken by age: I really do not know whether the essence of life is ambrosia or poison.

Subhashitarnava, 28

IF THE gods intend to crush a man they take away his good sense, so that he sees everything the wrong way.

Mahabharata, II, 72

THOSE BESET by cares find neither joy nor sleep; those tortured by hunger possess neither strength nor fire; those torn by greed have neither friend nor relation; those vexed by love know neither fear nor shame.

Subhashitarnava, 170

FLIES GO after open wounds, bees after flowers, good people after good qualities, mean people after faults.

Vriddha Canakya, 213

OIL POURED into water, a secret entrusted to a crook, a gift made to a worthy person, and knowledge transmitted to an intelligent person – these all spread out by themselves.

Vriddha Canakya, 14, 5

SOMEBODY WHOSE mind is decreasing is pleased with the past, a fool with the future, the clever person with the present.

Mahabharata, I, 81

WHAT USE is wealth not spent and enjoyed? What use is power not employed to dispel an enemy? What use is knowledge not engaged in noble deeds? What use is the Self, if it does not rein in the senses and control itself?

Mahabharata, XII, 309

MARRIAGE AND friendship can only be entered into by those with equal wealth and equal education, not between affluents and paupers.

Mahabharata, I, 122

ONE WHO is intent on living well should avoid these six: too much sleep, sloth, fear, anger, laziness and procrastination.

Mahabharata, V, 33

RENOUNCING ALL the various activities think thus: "I am Brahman – I am of the nature of *saccidananda* (reality, consciousness, bliss)." And then renounce even this!

Tejobindu Upanishad, VI, 107

NOBODY ON earth has ever seen the fruit of righteousness or unrighteousness; therefore aim at becoming powerful, since everything is given to those who have power.

Mahabharata, XII, 132

INDEX OF SOURCES